" It's all been a misunderstanding! "

May this little book bring you hope!

Anita

by

Anita Grant *AKA fan*

"It's all been a misunderstanding"

Dedicated to my children,

my most precious gift.

Contents

Introduction

This book is for all the men, women and children who have experienced abuse.

I hope it brings you hope, uplifts and empowers you!

I originally started to write this book on the evening after my Decree Absolute was granted. This was the first evening my children and I were free from the tyranny of the man I had once called my best friend and husband.

However, I stopped writing when the memories of the emotional, physical, sexual and financial abuse became too painful and the stress of further court proceedings increased.

Now, as years have gone by and the children have grown into the most thoughtful, fun loving and hardworking adults a parent could ever wish for, I can look back with hindsight and see beyond the darkness to the light of hope that guided me.

I have written my story for those who suffer abuse in its many forms. If you are one of those people, I want you to know that it can turn out all right in the end, but you have to get help!

- - - - -

Introduction

My children and I are grateful to so many people and they remain continually in our prayers.

My family, friends and church family have been our rock and the reason why my beautiful children are enjoying the future they deserve.

I am especially grateful to three special people who made this book possible.

My thankfulness to God the Father for His miraculous rescue and restoration is immeasurable.

Finally, to repay their many kindnesses, I would like to help the NSPCC, Witness and Victim Support, Independent Domestic Abuse Service (IDAS) and Woman's Aid with the proceeds from the sale of this book. These organisations are Guardian Angels to people fleeing domestic cruelty and violence. Without their care, tenacity and knowledge, my children and I would not be together now, flourishing and free.

Part One - Abused

We don't choose our parents or where we are born.

As we grow through childhood, we start to have hopes, dreams and ambitions.

The choices we make have consequences.

Some of these may be harmful or even deadly.

1   Childhood

I am hiding under a sideboard and the 'dongs' of the News at Ten tv programme ring out. I am a young girl, no one is hurting me – I just like being invisible.

This is one of the few childhood memories I have and the experience might explain how my life turned out!

I was born in the 1960s to 40-year-old parents. My mum had a bubble perm and wore 'A' line skirts; she had suffered with poor mental health all her life. Dad worked long hours at a local factory.

As a young child I understood the importance of not making a fuss and of staying out of the way so I didn't upset anybody and everything would be ok.

This approach and these behaviours became part of me and stayed with me through to adulthood.

I could see my dad's love for mum through the dark depressions and paranoia she suffered. I'd never experienced anyone lying to me and I had been taken to church from a young age.

These experiences shaped my values. Life was quite ordinary.

"It's all been a misunderstanding"

For a few years in the 1970s, punk rock and fashion provided an escape from the unremarkable life I had at home.

Church, well, that was a place you went to on a Sunday morning at 10:30 for an hour. You sat in the same pew, sang some hymns and then went home after saying, "Good morning, how are you?", "I'm fine, thank you. How are you?!" At least, that is what my younger self thought.

I had a sister who was much older than me who had moved out of our home by the time I was two years old. She was my earthly Guardian Angel right up to my middle age. When I was sixteen, through encouragement and guidance, she introduced me to the teachings of Christianity and Jesus. This was my saving grace, as my story will tell. Without the inner assurance that I am loved by God, I would have either ended up in a mental health hospital, or dead.

- - - - -

This verse from the Bible helped me believe that there was more to life than this small and isolated existence:

"'For I know the plans I have for you,' declares the Lord, 'Plans to prosper you and not harm you.
Plans to give you hope and a future.'"
(Jeremiah Chapter 29 Verse 11)

A prayer:

Dear Father God, Thank You so much for this beautiful world. Help me to be the goodness in the community where I live, even when life is a struggle. Amen

2   When my whole world changed

*I am all alone on a doorstep, watching an ambulance drive away
with my father inside it.*

I was in my late teens and out with my mum and dad for an evening
meal at my boyfriend's parent's house. He and I had been together
for four years and I had a really good relationship with his whole
family. His mum was such a good cook. My mum had never cooked
for me, so this was a real treat. We had just finished the starter of
melon and the main course of Sunday Roast was about to be served
up.

My dad had been coughing earlier in the evening. Suddenly the
coughing got worse and he started holding his chest. He said he
needed fresh air and went out of the door; but moments later he
came back in. He was grey and grasping his chest. I recognised the
signs; he'd survived a heart attack when I was six years old. I
screamed for an ambulance.

Desperate, I ran over the road to a house that I knew had two
nurses living in it. I thanked God they were in and they came
rushing over. I had hope for a moment.

"Oh dear," they whispered. "Where are his tablets?"

"It's all been a misunderstanding"

From the colour of my dad's face and his body movements, they knew what was happening. I looked in my dad's jacket pockets, there was nothing there... their faces fell.

This time he died right in front of our eyes and left me with my mum.

Mum sat frozen to the spot, dumbstruck. I went outside and one of the nurses found me,

"His pupils are dilated.....I am so sorry."

I had no response; my dad had been my solid rock in life. He fed and clothed me, made me laugh and loved me. He had died between his melon and his main course.

I looked to the sky. The song 'Away in a manger' came to mind. I had no idea what came over me, but I sang the song from my childhood and I came to these verses:

"I love Thee, Lord Jesus, look down from the sky and stay by my side 'til morning is nigh. Be near me, Lord Jesus I ask Thee to stay, close by me forever and love me, I pray. Bless all the dear children in Thy tender care and fit us for Heaven to live with Thee there."

It was down to me to ring my sister and tell her about our dad. She moaned like someone in physical pain. No other words were said, apart from:

"We are on our way."

She had been burdened for fourteen years, since the first heart attack, that she would receive a phone call telling her this news. She and her family lived a long way away, so they had to make such an awful long journey. My niece told me later that the journey had passed mainly in silence and my sister had held her hand the whole way.

The vicar said:

"He was a gentleman; a gentle man."

Over three hundred people came to our dad's funeral.

Mum became more of an empty shell than she had been before and had to be looked after all the time. I left my job to become her full time carer.

Strangely enough, isolated at home, I didn't feel alone. I was used to being completely independent with no one really speaking to me at home. With my sister's guidance, I had become a Christian and had Jesus as my companion. I thank God for that.

My relationship with my long-term boyfriend fell apart, but I had spiritual comfort and I loved my daily Bible readings. I used positive verses to say strengthening words over myself. These nourished me. This is more than can be said about the food I ate at that time - no one seemed to notice I was living off two pieces of fruit and a biscuit a day. Mum had microwave meals for one.

I didn't grieve for my dad. I just took comfort that he was at 'perfect peace' and had been relieved from the burden of my mum.

"It's all been a misunderstanding"

I know that is a horrible thing to say, but she had tried to take her own life twice and because of her bad lungs she'd had at least three episodes in hospital each year. Mum had been so ill physically and mentally all my life and I had been told to prepare myself for her death numerous times. I could only see her as a burden.

- - - - -

This verse from the Bible kept me sane and able to get out of bed and be happy.

"I can do all things through Christ who gives me strength"
(Philippians 4:13)

I imagined I was serving Jesus when I was with mum and this helped my love for her grow and see her as a human being who was suffering.

A prayer:

Dear God, Thank You so much that You are a good Father who will never hurt or abandon us. Please help me to look after the children in my care so they can learn to love and be resilient in troubling times.

Amen

3   Treading on eggshells

"You know what you are doing!"

I stood, frozen to the spot, with my mind whirling as to what I was supposed to have done wrong.

These are the words my mother often said, with menace in her voice, every time she thought anyone was doing something against her. I had merely handed her the newspaper. She then aggressively pointed at the corner of the paper- it had a slight crease in it.
To me it meant nothing. To her it was a sign of me rejecting her, which I wasn't!

I don't recall any conversations with my parents during my childhood. Much of the time they were either busy in the garden, out dancing (I was left alone from the age of eight), watching tv or sat behind a newspaper. Dad worked shifts; Mum did regular household chores on certain days and then sat in her armchair in the living room; silent, still and disengaged. Mum had always struggled with her mental health. I don't remember feeling sad or lonely. I just played alone for hours in my bedroom creating things out of scraps of cardboard and UHU glue.

Mum spent long periods of time away from home. I don't remember ever asking where she was but I can remember my sister taking me once to see her in a large room with lots of people in armchairs. She was knitting a pink cardigan for me and asked me to try it on. I liked it so much without the sleeves that I took it home that day!

When my dad was still with us, he cooked our food when he came home from work. Vesta Beef Curry or an omelette with two mushrooms and one egg were regulars. Saturday was a greasy, but tasty, fry up; Sunday was a sumptuous roast. This all changed when Dad died. I was working in a catering company and got my food there. Mum preferred microwave meals or I did the fry up on a Saturday and a chicken or pork Sunday dinner.

Weekends brought some light relief. Sometimes I would go to my sister's on my own. Sometimes I would go with mum and dad to my aunt and uncle's house in the countryside. Both of these occasions hold happy memories for me. My sister served delicious food, had the softest bed sheets and taught me how to embroider (precious time together). My niece was born when I was eleven and I enjoyed playing with her. At my aunt and uncle's house it was relaxed, we sat around bonfires, sang songs and the adults laughed as they played cards.

School holidays meant going with my sister to her work; sitting in the corner of her office and playing lots of games in my head. I had to be very quiet.

- - - - -

About ten months after dad died, I remember phoning my aunt. I was getting exasperated with my mum's strange behaviour and outlined a few incidents to explain what I was dealing with on my own:

- I had bought a new rubber in the shape of a Disney character. It was something whimsical. When I showed it to mum, her face turned like thunder and she snarled, "You know what you are doing!" I whisked the rubber away and it never came out again. It was only years later that I found out, for some reason, she hated Disney characters.

- One time when we came out of church, she looked at me, agitated, "Did you see the vicar's wife's eye shadow? She's obviously trying to tell me that my eye shadow is too thick." I hadn't even noticed the vicar's wife had eye shadow on. We hadn't been that close to speak to her. I just got mum in the car and drove home to cook Sunday dinner.

- Another time when I had hung the washing out, mum called me into the kitchen. Her face was stony and I could sense her fury, so I braced myself for another accusation. "Why have you hung the towels like that? You know what you are doing...." I frantically looked at the towels and could see nothing wrong. Mum continued, "The tags should go at the back and at the bottom! You just wanted the neighbours to know where we get our things from." I told her to stop being so silly because no neighbour was bothered about us or interested in where we had bought our towels. I changed the towels round to stop her fretting.

- Her voice was loaded with disgust when she called me a "trollop" for drying a pan with a tea towel instead with the dishcloth. That was the *only* way to dry pans apparently!

The final straw (the incident that had made me phone my aunt) followed my mum's return from a holiday with my aunt and their brother and his wife. I'd had a break from Mum's paranoia, but when she returned, she reeled off a list of things her brother's wife had supposedly done against her. On one occasion Mum had been wearing a skirt and her brother's wife had been wearing trousers. Mum had concluded that her brother's wife was making a point, that she should not have been wearing a skirt, and this made her angry.

My aunty sighed on the phone. She'd wondered when I would be in touch. I'd been shielded from mum's episodes of paranoia by my dad and sister. Now that my dad was gone, I was experiencing it all on my own. I was told to ring the doctor.

- - - - -

The doctor said mum should come and see him. He altered her tablets, but they made no difference.

One evening, I heard a strange gurgling sound and I found my mum in bed, barely conscious. She had attempted to kill herself with the tablets. I rang for the ambulance. When mum came round in the hospital, she said she didn't want to live without my dad and couldn't go on. They had been together for forty seven years. My heart ached for her.

Time in the mental health hospital and ECT (Electro Convulsive Therapy) helped mum enough for her to be allowed home, but for weeks on end she just wasn't functioning. She went through the motions of putting on her make-up, doing her hair, dusting furniture and then just sat watching tv for hours and hours.

Unfortunately, she made a second attempt to take her life by taking all the tablets with her bedtime drink. I found her again, in bed, and phoned for an ambulance. I was cross this time and shouted at her:

"Life is precious. Do you ever think about how my sister and I feel?"

Another period in the mental health hospital and ECT helped much better this time and a new combination of tablets made all the difference. She became more vibrant and had light behind her eyes; something I had never seen before. Mum was able to come home.

Things were a lot brighter for a couple of years. One day she decided she was going to bingo. She enjoyed bingo, playing cards with her sister and meeting up with friends on a Saturday night for a dance. We actually had conversations together for the first time in my life. It was such a relief.

Unfortunately it didn't last. Her regular doctor suggested changing mum's medicine as she was "doing so well" and he didn't want her to become addicted to the tablets she was taking. We begged him not to change them as mum was in her seventies and was enjoying her adapted life. He insisted.

"It's all been a misunderstanding"

Two weeks after the change the lights went out and Mum began her downward slide. She became the empty shell I was accustomed to living with. She stopped getting dressed in the morning and stopped doing everything else. I was furious with the doctor and told him. I had phoned him previously to tell him she was struggling, but was told to give the new tablets time to take effect. This time, I told him I couldn't cope and feared what she might do. He told me to take mum to the Accident and Emergency department at the hospital.

Poor mum was in her nighty, big coat and slippers. She couldn't walk so I managed to get her a wheelchair. The compassionate receptionist could see that mum was suffering and gave us a blanket. I had no idea what anyone would do. All we could do was wait. After six hours, we were told there was no room at the local mental health hospital until the next day. I had to take mum home again. It was a sleepless and anxious night.

Taking mum to the mental health hospital the next morning was the hardest thing to do. She was still partly aware of what was going on and was sobbing and begging me not to take her. I had to take deep breaths and was constantly praying for Jesus' strength and peace over both of us.

The times in the mental health hospital were difficult. On one occasion we were having a conversation. when she suddenly sat upright and asked what the date was. I told mum and her response was a shocked,

"Well where have I been?"

Mum had been completely unaware of her time in the hospital for six weeks! It took another six weeks for her to be well enough to come home.

This time the treatment worked completely and, as of the time of this book being published – several years after these events - she has not had another episode of paranoia or depression.

I have asked mum what she remembers of these troubled times and she says that she has no recollection of having treatment in hospital at any time.

For me, these experiences shaped a part of me. It was a part that learned to ignore name-calling and accusations, to absorb trials and trauma and, above all, a part of me that learned to deal with things myself and to not make a fuss.

Now, my mum and I have such a loving and happy relationship. She is our Prayer Warrior and covers me, my grown-up children and our wider family in prayer every night. A friend once said to me:

"Never underestimate the power of a praying grannie!"

Throughout these times, mum loved me to sing the songs, 'Abba Father' and 'I am a new creation'. Both these songs can offer the comfort of God's presence and hope of new life within us.

> Abba Father, Let Me Be
> Yours And Yours Alone.
> May My Will Forever Be
> Evermore Your Own.

"It's all been a misunderstanding"

Never Let My Heart Grow Cold,
Never Let Me Go.

Abba Father, Let Me Be
Yours And Yours Alone. [2]

***

I Am a new creation, no more in condemnation,
Here in the grace of God I stand.

My heart is overflowing; my love just keeps on growing,
Here in the grace of God I stand.

And I will praise You, Lord, yes I will praise You, Lord,
and I will sing of all that You have done.

A joy that knows no limit, a lightness in my spirit
Here in the grace of God I stand.

And I will Praise You, Lord, yes I will praise You, Lord,
and I will sing of all that You have done.

A joy that knows no limit, a lightness in my spirit
Here in the Grace of God I stand. X3

- - - - -

Treading on eggshells

This verse from the Bible strengthened me throughout this time:

"Have I not commanded you? Be strong and courageous. Do not be afraid; do not be discouraged, for the Lord your God will be with you wherever you go."
(Joshua Chapter 1 Verse 9)

A prayer:

Dear Jesus, You are the healer. Please come close to me in my struggles with mental health, so I can feel Your restorative presence. Thank You for Your unfailing love.

Amen

4   A charming knight in shining armour

*I am stood in the middle of a living room – it's decorated in very
1990's style – black ash furniture and chintz sofa. It belongs to me
and my new boyfriend and it is our house. I am shaking my head
because I just don't want to be here.*
*"How did I get I get myself in this mess?" I say, in desperation, to
myself.*

The next chapter of my life started in the late 1980s, when I got a part time job at the local supermarket. I had also been volunteering at the local primary school, where a teacher had recommended that I should get a qualification in working with children. At that time I was looking after mum, attending college and then, starting to earn money by working part-time at the local supermarket.

It was at the supermarket that I met my new boyfriend, who would later become my husband. All of the staff at the supermarket warned me not to go out with him:

"He's a womaniser"

"He'll hurt you."

I ignored the advice I was given by the well-meaning staff, thinking that he was different with me. I was swept off my feet by his attention, smiley face, charisma and sense of fun. He used to say,

"I have always wanted a nice Christian girl."

A charming knight in shining armour

I was flattered, as I had always been the girl who would hide in the background and shy away from attention.

My mum loved him, as he was handy around the house and even called her "Mother".

Mum was in and out of the local mental health hospitals, so when I was out with my new boyfriend - dancing at a nightclub or being driven to National Trust places - I felt free from the burden of mum. He told me he loved me early on and said I was his "princess". In the time after losing my dad, he made me feel special.

- - - - -

The manipulation and deception was subtle at the beginning of our relationship but spread steadily into every corner of my life.

- A few weeks in, he started suggesting I could go to church at different times as he wanted to take me out for the day. He reasoned that if I went to church, we would lose time together. I was flattered that someone wanted to spend time with me and taken in.
- He suggested that one of my friends wasn't being friendly, even though and I thought she was her normal self.
- He took me clothes shopping (I loved it), to get me "clothes that suited me better". I found this a bit strange as others had always complimented my dress sense – anyway - if he was spending his money on me I was happy to have the clothes, as the majority of mine had been bought from charity shops.
- If I caught him in one of his frequent lies and asked him about it, he would say, "It's been a misunderstanding." and then talk his way out of it so I believed him again.

"It's all been a misunderstanding"

The 'suggestion' from him to move in together, made me feel sick. It was one 'suggestion' too far. This was totally against my faith and I didn't want to, at all. This was very clear to me, but I felt powerless against his constant pressuring and his telling me that it 'made sense'.

I was now renting my own room in a house as mum's paranoia took me to breaking point. I couldn't live with her any more, but I did still see her every day to drive her to wherever she wanted to go.

I knew he wouldn't stop with this idea until I relented, because this was a pattern of behaviour that had crept in and become firmly established in our relationship.

At that time I was renting my own room in a shared house as mum's paranoia had taken me to breaking point. Although I did still see her every day to drive her to whenever she wanted to go, I couldn't live with her any more. A part of me did agree that we would save money by moving in together and so I gave in.

- - - - -

Within three months, I knew I had to get out.

He was a great home-maker and we entertained friends but his demands on me were relentless. I was walking on egg shells all the time because I didn't know when he would suddenly turn nasty and call me a "whore" or accuse me of seeing someone else. I wasn't and it had never even occurred to me to look elsewhere.

If I was crying after an accusation he would always say in an overly gentle voice,

"Oh come here, you know I only do this because I love you."

A charming knight in shining armour

My body would be completely rigid as his hands roamed around my body. He told me I had to forgive him and move on as that was what my faith told me to do. He was right, Jesus did say we have to forgive all – so I did. But this is a twisted view of Christianity, as I came to realise later, when I was free to talk to others about this poisonous situation. Jesus never asked us to stay in an abusive and dangerous relationship. On the outside I was smiling, but on the inside I was literally screaming:

"Help me get out of this tangled web of claustrophobic attention!"

I secretly planned, with a couple of family members, to move out when he was at work. It had to be that way as he would have talked at me until I had relented and agreed to stay. I packed up my belongings, left him a note to explain and moved to another flat.

This was at a time when mobile phones weren't freely available, so his response was to ring my mum constantly on the home phone and ask her where I was. Mum told me he was crying and begging her to help him get me back. She didn't know where I was, as I had purposely not told her. Then he went round my church friends' houses and even an elderly relative's place trying to convince them that he loved me. He told them that "it's all been a misunderstanding" and that he'd start to come to church with me. That he would become a Christian.

They got that message to me and I thought I would be faithful to God and help bring him to know the love of Christ. Indeed, he did come to church every Sunday and I eventually moved back with him; thinking he had changed his ways. We even used to read the Bible together. Looking back, he was building his weapons against me as he was finding the verses about forgiveness and the duties of a wife. We planned to get married.

- - - - -

Our wedding day was lovely with so many special memories. Everyone pulled out all the stops and, right there in that moment, I believed everything would work out. However, one moment made my heart sink. As I walked down the aisle, I was struck that not a single member of his family was there and only two of his school friends had showed up. He told me that it didn't mean anything and that we are making our own lovely family – that was what mattered.

- - - - -

A charming knight in shining armour

A verse from the song in the previous chapter helped me at this time:

"I am a new creation, no more in condemnation. Here in the grace of God I stand."

It gave me hope.

A prayer:

Dear God, I am sorry for ignoring Your inner voice of warning and the advice of concerned friends. Please help me when I struggle with my self-worth and please protect me from those who want to mistreat and harm me. Thank You for the promise that we can be a new creation in Your sight.

Amen

5   New life, a new start?

Being stitched up after the birth of our child was one thing, but having to be re-stitched because of a "wife's duty" was the start of my emotions being dead inside me. I knew I had to get through this and survive.

Any hope of a fresh start soon faded.

A week after our first child was born he told me that I had to look after one of our shops. I was on maternity leave from school at this point, but one of our employees had walked out. Our poor child had colic and would cry a lot. I had no choice and I was stuck in the shop. After the first day, I said I couldn't do it anymore, but the look on his face told me not to argue; keep my mouth shut and get on with it. Added to this my re-stitching had become infected as I wasn't able to sit and rest. The birth had been horrendous because my pubic bone had been split when our baby was born.

His bullying and manipulative behaviour had returned shortly after we got married and it became relentless. I was 'advised' what to wear, who I could meet with and warned to keep up the appearance of a happy family. Within the first month of our marriage he said he didn't need to go to church anymore, and neither did I. I knew not to argue. If I had confronted him I would have suffered and then he would have repeated his usual refrain:

"It's all just a misunderstanding. You know I want the best for us."

New life, a new start?

What he didn't know was that I prayed and sang hymns silently in my head and, when he was at work, I read my Bible. I even dared to go to church as much as I could while on maternity leave. I was part of a community of caring and happy people, where I felt I belonged. I knew if I was ever free from him again, this was the place I would come.

Our second child was born a few years later. I had accepted my lot. We did have some good times.

We were now living in a four bed detached house in a quiet village. My job was at the local school. He went from one managerial role to another; always leaving in suspicious circumstances, but miraculously getting a new job very quickly. Our shop had been sold by now. We had three holidays a year, two cars and three house extensions. I had no idea where the money came from as I wasn't allowed a joint bank account with him and when I asked how much money we had he'd reply:

"Why do you want to know how much money we have? Don't you trust me?"

Sometimes I was made to sign documents without being allowed to read them. I just kept praying for God's protection.

My mum loved my husband because of all the jobs he did, but she hadn't realised he was charming his way into her will. My dear sister could see I wasn't happy but didn't know what to do. So we all pretended that all was well and we all played happy families.

"It's all been a misunderstanding"

Paradoxically, he was a fabulous dad to the children when they were babies and toddlers. The danger that I had suffered for years came to them when they became three years old.

- - - - -

A Bible verse I turned to repeatedly was:

"And we know that in all things God works for the good of those who love Him, who have been called according to His purpose." (Romans Chapter 8 Verse 28).

My mistake was that God has never ever called us to stay in abusive situations. Never!

A prayer:

Dear God, I speak against the powers of darkness that aim to disrupt my relationships. Please bring in Your mighty power to heal and restore the brokenness. Thank You for the beauty found in genuine love and kindness.

Amen

6 My inner being is screaming, "Get us out, please get us out!"

A child is made to stand up on a stool and hold a glass near their mouth. Their dad has told them to and is holding a carving knife near the child's mouth. The glass is held ready to catch the blood from their tongue .

The dad is him, my husband, the child's father. The threat of cutting out one of his children's tongues is one of the horrific disciplining methods he used to shock and terrify us for many years.

When our first child started at nursery aged three, I made sure they knew how to write their name and the basic colours, shapes and numbers to ten. My husband thought this wasn't enough and demanded that they were reading, knew the ten times tables and much much more. Thankfully he had a job from 7am to 7pm and, in that time our first child achieved a lot. However, for his own protection, and to avoid punishment for not meeting the standard demanded, I made sure our first child was in bed before his father got home.

Our second child wasn't so lucky. My husband had lost another job and was at home in the daytime. I think he felt emasculated and status less. A good job title was vital to his prestige in the family and community. He was a really kind and playful dad up until each child reached the age of three. At this point, something switched inside him and he became a monster.

No one can learn if they don't feel safe. Our first child developed a stutter while reading because he was so frightened to make a mistake. This was because my husband believed that discipline, rather than respect and care, brought the best out in people. So he put a flip flop on the coffee table ready to hit the child if he made a mistake. I took the flip flop away time and time again, but then that ended up with him screaming in my face and the child begging him to stop. It was a no win situation.

There was a time when the children were playing nicely in the garden. They always played nicely, because we had to stick together. One was a horse and the other was riding on his back. My husband decided the one on the back was being horrid, so he dragged the child in, put both the child's hands behind their back, pinned the child to the floor and covered their mouth and nose so they couldn't breathe! I rushed in to find the child's eyes bulging and he was shouting:

"I will not have anyone bullying, this is what it feels like!"

I rushed at them and shoved my husband off our child. The poor thing was gasping for air and bright red. The child collapsed into a ball in my arms. The fear was palpable. My husband raged at me – he was so close to me that his spit was splattering my face. His fists were clenched so tight we braced ourselves for a beating. It didn't come.

My inner being is screaming, "Get us out, please get us out!"

I told the children to go back outside; I went back to what I had been doing. Then, within half an hour, he gathered us together and we were made to sit on the sofa with him and he declared in an affected caring voice:

"Now, we know that you children caused that upset to me and your mummy. But we forgive you because it was all just a misunderstanding."

The children sat with their eyes down. My brain and body were pulsing with rage and frustration. We said nothing until he said we could go.

He would also use belts and his hands on us if he thought we 'deserved' it.

The knives came out if he thought we were lying.

It started when the children were so small they couldn't see inside the top kitchen drawer. I know this, because the disciplining time would come when he asked the child to go and choose the knife he was to use on them. He would snarl:

"No one lies to me!"

Then he would drag the child on top of a stool, put a glass in their hand and get them to hold it near their mouth. He didn't want any blood going on the floor. The child stood motionless, their sibling and I were screaming in our heads:

"Please get us out, dear God get us out!"

He even, made the children put their head on a chopping block; with the threat of he would chop off their head if they defied him.

He never did cut them. He was too clever to have made marks that would have been seen by a teacher. The terror was enough to hold us prisoners in absolute fear of him. He loved his dominance, his family – his domain. It was a volatile, violent and unpredictable environment. When he had finished terrorising us, he would tell us it was all for the best of the family - "It was all a misunderstanding" and he "loved us" and then, he'd expect us to snuggle up on the settee with him. He just made light of it all.

It was all about mind games to him. He loved to do it to others. He once said with such a smug look on his face:

"I love to light a fire, then stand back and watch it burn."

It was noted at school that the children were sullen and cried when their dad picked them up. The school never shared that with an outside agency, or with me. (at least, not until a court case years later) The children never knew how their dad was going to be and just lived under a dark cloud of fear and oppression.

This all came out in the NSPCC counselling sessions after we were rescued and put in a safe house.

- - - - -

There were many incidences where he mentally, physically and verbally abused me. Far worse than this, watching my children being ill-treated, was torture.

My inner being is screaming, "Get us out, please get us out!"

He had decided our eldest child was getting a bit chubby. He told the child not to eat everything on the plate because he was getting fat. At the next meal, our eldest remembered what his father had told him, and left some of his meal. When my husband saw this he asked why he wasn't finishing his meal, the child told him. He swung his head to me and shouted,

"Oh, I see what you are doing....you're trying to undermine me!"

I explained that our child was only doing what his dad had told him to do. He then repeated the threatening phrase:

"You know what you are doing!"

He knew that phrase made my stomach churn, as it reminded me of what my mum used to say to me when she was ill.

On another occasion, we were having pasta and garlic bread for dinner. I put side plates out, as I always did. He looked at me and asked why I had put side plates out. I tried to make light of it and said it was for his bread. He told me not to be so stupid and that we didn't need them as it was extra washing up. Next time we had pasta and garlic bread, I didn't put side plates out. He swore at me when he got his garlic bread:

"Where the f____ am I meant to put this?"

I reiterated that he had told me not to put them out. He snarled:

"Oh you know what you are doing!"

"It's all been a misunderstanding"

I put side plates out after that. I was caring less and less about his outbursts and becoming increasingly numb inside.

Another of his threats would be delivered over the phone:

"I'll deal with you when I get home. Don't go to sleep."

He often came in after 3am. This was down to the shifts he worked in a new job. I had stayed awake through fear. Sometimes I went to work with only two hours sleep. I worked with a very compassionate colleague and she picked up on the sadness beneath my sunny veneer and would give me a hug. No words were spoken, she just knew.

Things were so dangerous at home for the children and me. We needed to get out and say "please help" to someone. He made it clear that, if I ever tried to leave, he would say I was mentally ill like my mother. He had the passports to take the children out of the country and told me I would never see them again.

- - - - -

My inner being is screaming, "Get us out, please get us out!"

This is the Bible verse I clung on to that reminder me I could cope.

"For God has not given us the spirit of fear; but of power, and of love, and of a sound mind."
(2 Timothy Chapter 1 Verse 7)

A prayer:

Dear God, I am sorry for the harm children suffer. Thank You for IDAS , NSPCC and all the other organisations that provide compassionate support and fight for the safety and protection for all.

Amen

7   The rescue and refuge

"Please, please just go away."

I beg the three policemen who have just come to our house in the night. I'm trying to shut the door on them. But one puts his foot in the way.

The violence and abuse really had escalated. The children were late primary age by now and we perpetually lived two lives. One for the outside world – happy, 'middle-class' family with all the luxuries; the other behind closed doors - just living to please my husband and trying to avoid anything that might lead to an outburst. Friends always remarked how well behaved the children were….they would not have dared to do anything that drew attention to themselves.

One ordinary evening a friend brought me news; what she called, "Your get out of jail free card." She had found proof of my husband having an affair.

It was not an unusual occurrence for my husband to have affairs. I'd known early on, but without proof, that he loved having the 'attention' of women and he was <u>charm</u>ing to them. He had even told a neighbour that he had given up eight women to be with me. I was reconciled to this demeaning situation. At least I didn't have to do my "wifely duties" quite so often; sometimes it was five times a day. I had learned to wash up at the kitchen sink or go up the stairs sideways because his hands would always be groping! Now that I had definite proof of his unfaithfulness, with my friend's help, I filed for divorce on the grounds of unreasonable behaviour and adultery.

Praying desperately for courage and God's protection for us all, I gave him the letter from the solicitor. It was like someone had punched him. I stood grounded to the spot, bracing myself for what would come. He just flopped down onto the settee and asked why. He looked crestfallen and told me that this home and lifestyle was all for me. I told him that I knew about his affairs and his bullying had gone on long enough.

I remember him saying:

"Oh come on, you know that I only want the best for you. It's all a misunderstanding. This so called 'friend' is not a friend if she is trying to break up our marriage!"

I pointed out that it was his behaviour and his adultery that is breaking up our marriage. His response was:

"Well, I don't know who's put you in a bad mood, but I'm not having it."

I could have torn my hair out in frustration at his complete dismissal of his behaviour. It was made out that I was mistaken and had got it all wrong! I started retaliating; I had got to a point that I couldn't care less if he hurt me. I used to say that I hated him and:

"It's all been a misunderstanding"

"I'd rather live in a shack, than live with you!"

His response was to ask who was telling me to say these nasty things!

Daily life with him became more tortuous as he followed me from room to room begging me to take back the divorce. I stood my ground. He had broken his marriage vows and the divorce was happening. Tragically, my husband was meddling with the children's minds as well. Telling them that mummy was breaking up our happy home and leaving them with him. Well that freaked them out and they became even more clingy to me. I reassured them that they will always be with me, wherever that may be. School must have noticed the children's demeanour.

- - - - -

Then about two weeks later, my husband went to work, as usual, in the evening and, as usual, the children and I breathed a sigh of relief. At about 10:30pm I got a call from him. He was very quiet and slurring his speech.

"I can't live without you, you know I love you, so I am going to a place where no one will find me."

I asked what he meant. He repeated the same words and made sobbing noises. I panicked. He sounded like my mum when she had taken her overdoses. I told him to come home and promised we would sort things out. (I hadn't realised at the time but my husband knew what voice to use as I had spoken about what had happened to mum.) He begged me to say "bye" to the children because he "couldn't make mummy happy" and put the phone down. I circled the living room like a caged animal. With my heart palpitating and saying, "what shall I do, what shall I do?" I rang his number several times but he didn't pick up. I rang my sister and the police.

The police came quickly and said they had traced his phone to a place in the city. I knew the area was near a river. I was going to pieces because I feared the trauma the children would suffer through this. I imagined that he had parked up and drowned himself. The police could see how frightened I was. My sister made cups of tea and sat holding me. The police phoned him several times before he picked up. They demanded that he came home.

I was told to go in another room, while they waited for my husband to come into the kitchen. After he arrived, we waited for about half an hour for one of the policeman to come through to us. His first words shook me; I literally felt my body judder.

"He's a control freak! We've told him to behave himself and accept the marriage is over. We know that it is not 'a misunderstanding', as he keeps telling us, it's real!"

My husband had told them that I had mental health issues like my mother and I was going through a breakdown. They didn't believe a word he said and could see right through to his abusive core.

They police left, as did my sister (very reluctantly), and we went to bed saying nothing.

A hushed, oppressive calm came over the house for a while; I went to work, the children went to school and he became kind and apologetic. Saying he had just been trying to make a great family, because family is all that mattered. I sort of understood how this family was so important to him. His own childhood had been horrid, and there were marks on his back that showed he had been whipped. Then his dad had died and I started feeling sorry for him, I even found him reading the Bible.

- - - - -

However, it didn't take long before he went back to his usual manipulative and abusive self, telling the children:

"If Mummy ever leaves me, I will kill myself."

This tortured their young minds.

Then came my husband's relentless following and begging me to stop the divorce, until one morning it stopped.

I was in the shower and, as usual, he was stood outside the shower door talking at me to keep the family together. I had to forgive him as Jesus would want me to - "Family is all that matters." I felt all my resolve inside me crumble and I relented. I said I would stop the divorce and try again on the condition that certain behaviours and the other women had to stop. He agreed.

My husband was so thrilled, that he opened the shower door and told me to get dressed so we could tell some neighbours we were together again and going to make it work. The depression inside me was choking. With my hair still wet, he took a bottle of champagne to the neighbours so we could "celebrate"! When they opened the door their faces lit up and invited us in. They chatted away about how the children would be delighted mummy had changed her mind. In my head, I'm thinking – can't you see my smile is fixed and my whole demeanour is one of someone who is broken. The children just accepted what was going on. They explained, years later, that they had just tuned out from what was going on and played in their own worlds. This is heart breaking.

My sister was distraught that I had stopped the divorce. I tried to reassure her that all would be well and "family is everything to fight for". (I realised I was using my husband's words to reassure myself.) People at work said they admired me for trying again. Inside I am clinging on to my sanity with my fingertips and a smile on my face. In error I consoled myself that I was doing it for Jesus because my husband would to come to know Him. My sister couldn't cope with this and distanced herself away because she knew how much my husband loathed her and she didn't want to enrage him.

- - - - -

It didn't take long for my husband to go back to his default setting of abuse and manipulation. The children and I existed. He had now taken to accusing my sister of interfering and it was all her fault that our marriage and family were falling apart. I hadn't even spoken to her for quite some time. It all came to a head one evening when I was making dinner.

I was in the corner of the kitchen worktop making coleslaw. He was right in my face growling about how my sister was poison and she needed to go away. I pointed out that I hadn't seen my sister and that it was his nastiness to us that was the problem.

"We do what we were told to do and don't deserve this treatment," I pleaded.

He was so close to me by then that his words spat in my face, I snapped and slapped his face to make him move back – the first time I had retaliated in eighteen years of being together! He slapped me back – not the first time he had hit me.

Horror happened again, my husband then went to grab me, but as he did, the bowl of coleslaw flung up and hit the kitchen ceiling. I am screaming now because he has taken my arm and twisted it round my back and grabbed my hair and was bashing my face on the floor. I thought my shoulder was going to come out of its socket. I looked at the kitchen door. Thankfully it was shut so the children couldn't see, but of course they could hear... They heard him say,

"You deserve this you whore. If only you would do as you are told. You're just hurting yourself."

I struggled him off and grabbed a chair to put between me and him. He told the children to get help from a neighbour.

When they walked in, they saw me bright red in the face, hair all over the place and shaking holding the chair. Some of the coleslaw was still on the ceiling and some was on the floor. I must admit, to them I looked a mess.

"I just don't know what to do with her, just look at her, she's mentally ill like her mother and I don't know why she does it," my husband told the neighbours.

He came over to me and stroked my arm like he was being a tender spouse.

I was speechless as I saw a scene play out in front of me that doesn't match what the children and I have just been through. The neighbours set about getting dinner for the children that I had prepared. I tried to explain what had happened – surely they saw his hand print across my face, as it was still stinging. Their answer was that I shouldn't have slapped him in the first place. If I didn't have the power of God in me, I would have gone into deep depression.

All through dinner I wanted to really hurt him, I was seething. Then my husband got me and the children to sit on the settee. He got his arms around us and tried to make us into a big huddle. We were stiff with anxiety:

"Everything will be ok. Our family is together. It's just been a misunderstanding. But Mummy knows she has to forgive me 'cos Jesus said so."

I caught the children's eyes. They were dull and frightened, looking at me to 'stop all of this'. He then went to work and we were safe for a few hours. It sounds awful and all so wrong now, but the children and I knew just to get on and go about our routines because we saw no way out. I even found myself saying sometimes,

"It's all been a misunderstanding"

"Daddy didn't mean it." That is so, so wrong!

- - - - -

The next day, we played 'happy families' and went to a friend's house together. While making the tea, my friend called me into her kitchen. I had my long sleeve cardigan on, even though it was really hot. She looked me in the eyes, stroked my face where he had slapped me and quietly asked,

"When are you going to say – that's enough!?"

I slightly shook my head and my eyes pleaded with her not to say anything. So we served the tea and cake. All of us had a happy time in that sanctuary of her house.

When my husband had gone to work in the evening, my niece came round. I told her what had happened. She insisted I rang the police.

"This is not normal. You have to stop this because he won't."

I gave all the reasons I couldn't. She gave me all the reasons I could.

I summoned up all the courage I had and reported the incident to the police, plus how he used knives, belts, suffocation and shoes on us. Also, that he emotionally and financially abused us. The phone operator said I needed to come in and give a statement. I insisted I couldn't but please could she log my call. She did, but reiterated that we were in danger and I was to come in the next morning and make a statement. I said yes, but I knew in my heart I just couldn't. I truly feared the consequences.

So I went to bed. I sat up against the pillows and stared around the bedroom, it was pitch black.

"I can't do this anymore!"

I cried in my prayers and just sat there.

What happened next will defy all common sense and reason.

As I looked at my husband's side of the bed (he was still at work), I could see my dad as clear as anything! Yet, he had died years earlier. He was sat on the bed with his back against the pillow and his feet up; he had on the clothes I remember him wearing, even his tie and a big smile on his face. I could see the mark on his front tooth where he'd been hit by a cricket ball. Nothing was said, but a deep sense of calm and peace came over me. I didn't move but I looked him in the eye; he kept smiling. I blinked and he was gone. My mind couldn't quite comprehend what had happened, it felt so normal, but wonderful at the same time. I went to sleep. Thankfully, I was blessed with restful sleep whenever I was alone and my head hit the pillow.

The next thing I know is there is loud knocking on the front door. I get my dressing gown on and go to the door. I could see blue lights flashing through the glass. My heart starts pumping. As I opened the door and my mind was spinning; it was three police officers. My immediate thought was that my husband had actually carried out the threat to kill himself and they had come to tell me.

Then I realised that their mouths weren't saying that, so I had to ask them to say what they had just said again.

"It's all been a misunderstanding"

"We have heard your phone call earlier this evening, we know of your husband and if you don't get out, you will be dead."

I couldn't grasp this and the fear of my husband coming home took over me.

"Please, please just go away,"

I begged to them. I tried to shut the door on them, but the nearest one put his foot in the way.

"Please go away, my husband will come back and you are making a noise."

"You had better let us in then," said the officer.

I put my body in the way of the door.

"It happens in middle class you know," said another officer.

That sentence was enough to halt me in my tracks. I stood with my hand on the doorframe. I started to sob uncontrollably:

"Do you mean you believe me?" My guard was down.

When they came in, one radioed to control that they were in the house and another got his note book out. One stood near the door. I asked them to be quiet so as not to wake the children.

I was told that my husband was being arrested over the next few minutes and we were safe. I got the neighbour who had seen the 'coleslaw' incident to hear what the police had to say. For the next three hours I was questioned. They gave me a leaflet for a Domestic

Violence Refuge and would be back in the morning, after they had questioned my husband. My neighbour's face showed she didn't believe a word I said but I thanked her for being there.

Needless to say, I didn't sleep. At 6:30am I rang my sister. She was with us by 7am. By this time the children were up and totally oblivious to the events that had occurred. We had breakfast together. While they played in the playroom, I explained to my sister what had happened, including the mysterious event of me seeing our dad on my bed. She thought about that for a bit and replied,

"Angels come in all shapes and sizes. God knew you had come to the end of yourself."

We then carefully explained to the children that the police had been talking to daddy about what he had done to us and they are not happy him. It's hard to know what they truly thought, but there were no tears or questions about what would happen to their dad. In fact, as the months and years after this event rolled by, they never asked to see him ever again. It proved that they never had a relationship with him. This did break my heart, as we could have had an amazing family, if only he hadn't hurt us. I often asked why he did what he did and his response was that he knew best for us. For now, we would live somewhere else free from his menacing behaviour.

Later that morning, the police contacted us to say my husband had been interviewed and would be charged, but he would be released over the next hour. That sent us into panic mode. I immediately rang the refuge number for their help. I had to wait for them to ring back once they had sorted out a place for us. In the meantime, me and my sister grabbed dustbin liners (the cases were in the loft) filled them with some clothes, quilts, pillows, toiletries and a few toys. My sister also threw the contents of the fruit bowl into a bag and we left our 'home'......forever!

We had to meet a representative from the refuge at a certain place. So we waited there. Thank goodness I had a mobile phone at that time. I rang our village vicar to tell her what was going on. She asked me where we were. She came and gave me £100 cash! I was so grateful as I had £12 in the bank and only a few pounds in my purse. In all the rush to get out we hadn't had lunch. So when the refuge representative came, the vicar asked them to take us to a McDonald's on the way as we were hungry.

The refuge lady was so kind and had an air of efficiency about her that I immediately felt better. She told me where we were going and I was to follow her. We drove for over forty minutes and pulled up outside a building that made us feel quite apprehensive. However, it was a place I knew my husband wouldn't find and it had a door we could lock. She apologised that there hadn't been time to clean the apartment, but we would be safe here, and that she would be back in the morning, as would another police officer. She gave us a hug and a lovely smile – we certainly needed that!

The children and I looked around and it was a nice enough place, but it didn't have the heating on or hot water. We were exhausted and cold, so after a bit of fruit, we snuggled up in the same bedroom to try and get some sleep. We had brought our own quilts thankfully. Unfortunately, there was no toilet roll and one of the children had a bout of diarrhoea. The poor child suffered quite a bit. I had to clean them up with some clothes I had brought. I had to leave the clothes soaking in the bath with cold water as I had nothing else. We were grateful for the rescue, but these first twenty four hours were a nightmare. I prayed for God to make it all better.

A policeman came at 8am to interview me about my husband's demands on me:

> "Tell me about the details of the alleged rape your husband carried out against you."

That was the first time I'd been confronted with *that* word; I'd always called it my "wifely duties".

We'd been speaking for a while, when he stopped and suggested we had a cup of tea. I said I had nothing and told him about the diarrhoea episode last night and that we had no toilet rolls, heating or hot water. We only had the bag of fruit we had brought with us. He was so very kind and went to the shop and got us some provisions to keep us going for a couple of days. The children and I were so thankful for his thoughtfulness and thoroughly enjoyed a hot drink. It warmed our cold bones.

When he'd gone, the lady from the refuge came and got the heating and hot water sorted out and we got nice and clean. My niece even managed to get a couple of throws to put over the settees and a couple of ornaments to make things more homely. My sister got a mobile phone charger to me, as I'd forgotten mine in the rush to get out. The phone miraculously had lasted on five percent charge for two days! The Domestic Violence team looked after us well and kept my sister up to date with what was going on. We felt looked after and knew we could contact them any time.

Throughout all this, the children trusted me to take care of them. I don't fully know why – poor lambs. I made sure I told them the truth, on a 'need to know' basis and I kept being smiley. Making sure my face and voice said – it's ok, we are being helped. We lived our lives as a unit. We held onto each other, weeping and shaking many times. The refuge was our happy place of safety. It was a bit of a dump, but it was Our Dump!

- - - - -

The Bible verses from Psalm 46 gave me an inner comfort and strength and came true in the end.

"God is our refuge and strength, an ever-present help in trouble. God is within her, she will not fall; God will help her at break of day. He says, "Be still, and know that I am God."

A prayer:

Dear Father God, thank You for Your heavenly power breaking through into this earth to rescue us. Thank You for the police and the organisations that are there to help those who are living with abuse. Please give me courage to all overcome the fear of those who are abusing me.

Amen

Part Two - Rescued

I wish I could say that the next part was easy - our turn to have freedom in peace - but I can't.

Throughout it all, we had the invaluable guidance and support of Women's Aid, IDAS, Victim Support and the NSPCC. I hope you can see how they can be there for you too.

My companion throughout all these trials was, and is today, Jesus.

This is what happened next.

I've segmented it into the different areas we experienced.

"It's all been a misunderstanding"

"Forget the former things; do not dwell on the past. See I am doing a new thing! Now it springs up; do you not perceive it: I am making a way in the desert and streams in the waste land."
(Isaiah Chapter 43 Verses 18 and 19)

Even though this Bible verse was speaking in pictures, I took hope that restoring and renewing times were coming.

8 "It can't have been that bad, you would have left ages ago!"

These were the words of a so-called 'friend' of mine who had just seen the local newspaper. They had released details of the harassment court case that the children and I had been through. The front page had a photograph of my face, and that of a police officer, with the headline –

"Ex-husband charged with harassment".

The children and I were now living, with the help of the Benefits System, in a 'two-up two-down' rented house. A blessed gift.

THE HARASSMENT

For three weeks after we were rescued and placed in a refuge, we had no contact from my husband. We had an eerie sense of quiet and calm. Naively, I thought my husband had relented – maybe we should have left years earlier? Then came the 'storm'!

It was a good job we had a small but very supportive and loving network of people around us. The following five years would see us go through twenty six court cases – Family Court for the children and divorce; Magistrates Court for the harassment; Crown Court for the abuse, compensation claims and on-going child maintenance struggles. These court cases were the ever-present backdrop to the daily challenges we faced.

At this point, the district judge of the Family Court had ordered that my husband could only see the children under supervised contact.

The following table catalogues the harassment. The boxes that contain my husband's false allegations against me show he totally wasted police and other officials' time. The incidents often coincided with a time when he had lost one of the many battles he waged against the children and me.

"It can't have been that bad, you would have left ages ago!"

WHEN	INCIDENTS	CONSEQUENCES
Three weeks after we were rescued. On a weekly and, sometimes daily basis; continuing for over three years	I received intimidating anonymous BT payphone texts (more than ten) saying a bomb would be set off, people coming to get me, the children would be killed (the police traced them all to him), endless begging letters (sometimes five a day), coming on to my property, pestering elderly relatives and friends to make me go back to him, silent phone calls, threats to take the children out of the country, threatening to kill himself.	Panic alarm given to me. My husband given 12 months conditional discharge in the Magistrate's Court. With the judge commenting that my husband had to accept the marriage was over and behave with decency. turned to use the civil judicial system and police to continue indirect harassment.
Six months after we were rescued	My husband makes false allegations that I am racially harassing him with the help of my family – racist taunts, stones being thrown in the night at the matrimonial house windows, following him, ringing and texting him. When offered a CCTV at house he refused!	Because no evidence was found, my husband complained to five different police stations, he got Inspectors and Cultural Diversity involved. He was told no further action (NFA)! He had now got himself a reputation for being a pest to the police authorities.
A month after previous incident	My husband approached the children and their friends at the front of our rented house. The children were	This was not handled properly by the police. The children would play in the back garden from that day onwards.

	terrified and ran inside crying.	
A week after previous incident	My husband broke his bail conditions by sending a letter directly to my house. All his letters should have gone through his solicitors.	My husband was arrested and put in cell for a night.
Three days after the previous incident	My husband makes false allegations that I am intercepting his mail with help of a post lady.	The post lady kept her job as the police investigation showed no evidence. NFA. This was revenge against me because a letter addressed to both of us had come to me by redirection of mail and it showed that he had six aliases– so I reported this to the police and the Tax Office; they then, must have investigated him.
Eight months after we were rescued	He was questioned about child cruelty. He didn't turn up for first appointment, then he was given a new date for the next month, but didn't turn up again because he was on holiday! He was eventually interviewed ten months after we were rescued. He is on his third solicitor.	My husband was charged with neglect and child cruelty. He complained that he was being racially harassed by the police! However, if he had turned up to the previous two dates for interview, the police would not have had to keep contacting him.
Over a period of 6 months in	My husband makes false allegations that I have abused the children.	No evidence was found. (NFA) The police said it was a scurrilous

"It can't have been that bad, you would have left ages ago!"

the year after the rescue		attempt by him to defame my reputation. But it halted child cruelty case for seven months.
Two years after the rescue	After being ordered out of the matrimonial home by a County Court Judge, my husband caused excessive, threatening and blasphemous damage; including the kitchen ceiling falling down due to an upstairs leak he'd caused.	He wasn't charged as he did this while he still occupied it - "a person can do whatever they wish when they are in their own home!" Police told me this, but they did take photographs that I used in the court cases for the children.
Two years and two months after the rescue	I had to report some more of my husband's harassment to the police as my husband was harassing the Estate Agents to hamper the sale.	We lost £75,000 from the original price of the house due to the damage my husband caused. This was an own goal for him – if he had sold two years previous, he would have been financially better off.
At the time of me trying to sell the house	My mum, sister and I receive numerous silent or offensive/threatening phone calls.	Logged at control room
Two and a half years after the rescue	On the same day my husband was at the magistrate's court committal hearing for Child Cruelty –	Logged at control room

	my sister receives a silent phone call. He is now on with his fifth solicitor.	
Two months after the above incident	Mum receives four anonymous crude phone calls.	Logged at control room
Three years to the date after our rescue	The children and I are walking in a street near our rented house, when my husband stops his car to stare at us and talks animatedly on his mobile phone.	Didn't report as I felt there was no point. He would have loved the thought that he had upset us and I didn't want to instigate another court case
Three years after our rescue	My husband takes photo of me leaving church.	Logged at police control room. No action taken by the police
Over a four year period after our rescue	My credit file showed he was trying to obtain money by using joint names as shown on Credit File – Experian. Including a CIFAS category 4, which indicates to any lender that at some stage in the past someone has attempted to obtain credit by fraudulent means.	Police say : "It's up to the banks to press charges"
Three and a half years after our rescue	I was investigated by the City Council Fraud Dept. My husband had made false claims that I had a partner called Mr Walker living with me, also that I claimed benefits I was not entitled	A fraud officer investigated fully and I am found completely innocent. NFA. To the day of me writing this book, I still have not had a new

	to and I earned £35k with a home party plan job, as well as my job at school.	partner. I have not had the courage.
Three and a half years after our rescue	He takes photo of me leaving church	A lady from the meeting escorted me to my car. She saw what he did. Didn't report – no point
Three years and nine months after our rescue	My husband makes false allegations that I have been harassing him at his taxi rank and he had witnesses. He had changed his name four times in the course of this time.	The Domestic Violence Unit put all his names in same system so if he rings to complain about me the operator can see his harassing behaviour.

There were many professionals involved in our lives during these years, supporting us in different ways and for this we are extremely grateful. There were four particular police officers in two counties that believed us and became our advocates. I wish I could mention their names because they went above the call of duty many times. They know how indebted we are to them and their humanity.

I was also granted 'special measures' for when I went through any of the court hearings. This means you are separated from the abuser in waiting rooms and court rooms and an advocate (Women's Aid, IDAS or Witness Support) can stay near you.

- - - - -

"It's all been a misunderstanding"

When these incidences were happening, Psalm 40:13-16 helped
me express my anger and find solace.

"Be pleased to save me, Lord; come quickly, Lord, to help me. May
all who want to take my life be put to shame and confusion; may
all who desire my ruin be turned back in disgrace. May those who
say to me, 'Aha! Aha!' be appalled at their own shame. But may
all who seek You rejoice and be glad in You; may those who long
for Your saving help always say, 'The Lord is great!'"

9   Free at Forty!

I had a dream of being forty years old and free of my husband and his abuse.

At the time of our rescue I was thirty-eight, so I thought this would happen easily. Little did I know how fiercely and deceitfully my husband would fight the divorce and for the custody of the children.

DIVORCE

I'd never experienced divorce or custody issues before so I had no idea what to expect but I knew I would need a solicitor.

We had a solicitor that my whole family had used for years for wills and other small legal matters. I went back to him to start divorce proceedings for the second time. Unfortunately, I was told that I couldn't use him as there would be a conflict of interest – my husband had already started custody and residency proceedings against me! My family and I were furious because he could have employed any solicitor in the city to represent him. This was an early sign of the devious manner in which he would continue to conduct himself.

Our family solicitor recommended someone else and my husband was issued with divorce papers again. Unfortunately, this coincided with me receiving papers from his solicitor for Residency and

Custody of the children. As the tangled mesh of the court proceedings became overwhelming, I was immensely grateful to have the support of a lovely lady from IDAS.

Including an essential change in solicitor, it took a year and seven months to get divorced.

My husband did everything he could to disrupt and stall the proceedings. Initially, he claimed we could solve the divorce through mediation. When the mediators heard what he had done to us, they told him it wasn't possible.

Thankfully, the district judge presiding over our case was meticulous in gathering and assessing the evidence from us both.

Because my husband was self-employed (he'd been fired from his last three jobs) the judge had a difficult time finding out his income. The earnings that he gave the HMRC did not match the house, lifestyle and cars we had. However, the judge followed the trail of cash going into his account – sometimes thousands a day! The judge kept asking for other bank statements where money had been transferred to and from. At one point my husband claimed it was a family member who was giving him the cash. That wasn't true, as that person was unemployed and had never had a job. The more my husband changed the booked court dates and the more he tried to bluff his way out of being fair to me and the children, the more the judge persisted.

My husband definitely had some income coming in as the mortgage was £7,500 in credit and it emerged that he was getting Child Tax Credits paid into his bank account. He had actually put one of the children down as being disabled – which they weren't – and he got extra money for that.

The final divorce hearing lasted three days. On the last day, when the judge came in the room, the first thing he said was:

"It's a dangerous thing to leave bank statements with a judge over night!"

The judge knew my husband was hiding money and could not be trusted to pay child maintenance, so he awarded us 87.5% of all the divorce money!! The money would come from the sale of the matrimonial house.

- - - - - -

As everyone expected, he refused to move out and the mortgage was in such credit that he didn't have to pay anything for two years. Eventually, another court order was made, and with police involvement, he did move out, although not without a final 'fanfare'!

He told his solicitor (his fourth) that he had booby trapped the house. His solicitor phoned my solicitor and warned me to take police with me when we returned to inspect property. On the day I got the keys, I took a friend from school and two police officers came with us. My husband was probably bluffing, but the police knew the kind of man that he was and they were not willing to let us take the risk and return unaccompanied. We went to the house when it was dark to avoid being seen by the neighbours and giving them something to gossip about.

"It's all been a misunderstanding"

The police went in first of all, looking for booby traps or anything that could harm us. When the police gave the all clear, my friend and I entered the house. We kept the lights off and used torches to explore. When we went into the living room we saw all furniture was gone, apart from a beautiful painting on the wall I had always loved. My husband had written in thick black pen –

"Jesus loves you like f—k he does".

- and scribbled the dates of some of the court hearings we had been to. I called out to the police, they were in the kitchen, to ask if they had seen the picture. One of the officers called back:

"Mm, you obviously haven't seen this! The guy's an absolute nutter!"

My heart sank. I tentatively went into the kitchen; both police officers were shining their torches on a large wall (about 5m by 2m). We all stood in stunned silence. What greeted us was something like a graffiti wall. My husband, with a thick black pen, had covered the wall with A5 size drawn rectangles, each bearing a woman's name with a year written underneath. I assumed this was him bragging about all the affairs he had had while we were married. Each rectangle had a nail hammered into the wall like a picture frame! He'd also inexplicably drawn twenty one coffins and written:

"I have been killed twenty one times, but I still keep getting up".

He had also drawn a picture of me naked, with "you will never win" written across my stomach. I stood there speechless, I could only think how blessed we were to be away from this man! Thank God for those police officers who, two years previously, had taken the decision to get us out!

Every room had been stripped of all furniture and had some damage done to it; wallpaper ripped, tiles smashed, windows smashed, wires torn from the walls and paint damaged. Faeces had been smeared on the childrens' bedroom walls. Every plant pot in the garden had been smashed.

One thing we didn't notice until about a week later was that he had left the upstairs shower running ever so slightly down the wall. It leaked into the kitchen and caused the ceiling to collapse.

Thankfully, I had taken insurance out so the damage was covered. I spent whatever time I could getting the house back to saleable condition again. It had been a beautiful house.

My husband's actions wiped £75,000 off the sale price of the house....a bit of an own goal for him. His share of the divorce -12.5% wasn't going to get him much. I was able to pay back my lovely nephew so he could now buy his first home.

I regret not showing the neighbours the damage my husband caused. I could have said:

"See....this is the true character of the man!" But I didn't.

They fully supported him and still think I am the nasty one who tore his family apart. For our part, the children and I have focussed on the most faithful and supportive family and friends who remain in our lives to this day. Those who couldn't see our suffering and, in supporting him, went against us are the ones who have missed out on being part of the children's lives and watching them flourish.

The children never saw the damage to our home; they had enough bad memories already.

- - - - -

They say, "time is a healer."

I can remember the moment I felt a shift in my brain. For nearly twenty years, the time I had been with my husband, I'd felt I had to have two brains: one for the here and now and one to anticipate anything that could anger him. It was three years after our rescue that I felt my brain becoming one entity again. It was the tremendous and invaluable support of IDAS, Women's Aid and the NSPCC that enabled this to happen.

Socrates explained that to live in grace:

"May the outward and the inner man become one."

We were now living in grace.

As to whether I achieved my dream....... I got my Decree Absolute two weeks before my fortieth birthday – I was free and forty!

On the journey to freedom I learned:

- Always tell the truth and have integrity.

- Remember all the agencies – IDAS, NSPCC, Witness Support, Women's Aid – are there to help you.
- If a Family Court judge has made a Residence and Contact court order in your favour, schools need a copy of it as soon as possible. This will let the Head Teacher know who has parental rights and gives them the power to turn the abusive parent away, should they turn up to collect the children without permission.
- Watch the words you are saying to yourself. They can harm your well-being. I used to say, "I'll never be free of him!" until someone pointed out that it could become a self-fulfilling prophecy. So I changed it to "Free at forty!"
- Remember you are of value and worth; precious in God's sight. (1 John 3:1a)
- Don't give in to pressure to accept all the legal deals offered through the proceedings. Some solicitors want things to be over quickly and may ask you to take a poor deal to get things finished.
- Ask the advice of others who are level headed before making decisions.

- - - - -

"It's all been a misunderstanding"

I was in a concert when I received the phone call from my solicitor to say I was legally divorced. The actual song that was playing at that moment had the words:

"My chains fell off, my heart is free, I'm alive to live for You!"

I held the phone out for my solicitor to hear. We laughed and cried together!

A prayer:

Dear Jesus, thank You, that by Your grace and forgiveness, we are now finally free. Please inspire a powerful programme of teaching the young about what a positive relationship is and how to have a feeling of self-worth as part of Your creation.

Amen

10 Protecting my children; my most precious gift

I'm watching the children play freely in the back garden of our new rented house and I know we are on the road to recovery and a brighter future.

FAMILY COURT

The fight through the courts to keep the children safe from my husband's abuse took five years. I had a 'guardian angel' from Women' s Aid and IDAS throughout these times and the children and I had the unrivalled support and counselling from the NSPCC. They were a soothing balm.

The thing I need to point out at this moment is that, since the rescue, the teachers noticed such an improvement in the children's demeanour and attainment. They said it was so marked and beautiful to see. Even though we were travelling forty minutes from the safe house to school on week days and we hardly had any possessions or clothes, we were feeling happier and lighter. We knew we were safe either at the refuge or school.

Life was wonderful on one level, on another it was total fear, chaos and frustration! But the children didn't need to know that. That was my job; their job was to have a childhood!

If you are living with abuse now, the following could unnerve you, but I ask that you keep reading, learn from my mistakes and go through the processes you need to - to be safe and happy for the *rest of your life*. Get help, you don't need to do it on your own.

It was when I reinstated the divorce proceedings that my husband brought Residency and Contact proceedings against me for the children. He even said, through his solicitor, that if I delayed the divorce for two years he would withdraw his claim for the children. This meddling delayed things for seven months but eventually the divorce proceedings went ahead!

A social worker came to interview the children at school within two weeks of our rescue. They spoke of what had happened to them and what they had seen and heard happen to me. I hadn't realised that my abuse would be taken into account as part of the harm done to the children. (There is a law case called 'Re:L' that states if a child witnesses abuse done to another, it is still classed as harm to them and the perpetrator can be prosecuted for it.)

Despite my police interview and the children's statements, my husband wasn't formally charged for his abuse against us at this stage "due to insufficient evidence". I was horrified. I had assumed a police investigation would find things. I realise now that I should have pointed the police in the direction to find the evidence. There were doctor's notes and the social worker's recommendations that were not taken into account and, on the night the police came to rescue us, they would have seen the physical marks on my face and arms if they had looked. I now know my husband was making claims against the police officers if they had dared to charge him.

The police just took the opinion that the children and I were now out of harm's way, so all would work out! Little did they know this would go on for a further three years of criminal proceedings and for five years in the Family Court!

About three weeks after our rescue, the social worker had taken the children to our former house and supervised the visit with their dad. It was noted that the children stayed together, were subdued and only gave him monosyllable answers. The social worker also noted that my husband wasn't interested in how they were and didn't even say sorry for what he had done. He just wanted to know where we lived. He kept whispering in their ears and the social worker asked him to stop. The detailed account of his behaviour was submitted ready for the Family Court paperwork. As soon as they came back to school from being with him, I was filled with relief:

"Right children, that's done now, let's go back to The Dump for tea."

We sang songs together in the car to pass the time.

In the first Family Court hearing, the judge noted the social worker's concerns and the severe things my husband had done to us. The judge ordered that he could see the children at a supervised contact centre. My sister and a lady from Women's Aid came for moral support. The Family Court room was less imposing than I thought; it was just a big room with a big desk and chairs around it. The judge, in a normal suit and tie, sat on one side and I sat at the other with my solicitor and my husband with his. The most intimidating thing that gave me the 'heart in my mouth' feeling was being in the same room as *him*. I used to take a notebook and pen and write down all that was said and by whom. This was a valuable technique that helped me keep calm and, when the panic had subsided, once back at home, I could go over the notes and refresh my memory of what was said and prepare to fight any lies or misconceptions in the next court hearing.

By this time, my husband had been charged with harassment. His claim of, "It's all been a misunderstanding" had lost all its power!

The first supervised contact was a disaster; the children didn't want to go and were crying. However, under the suggestion of the social worker, they did go with a family friend. I don't know what happened there but the children were clear about not wanting to see their dad anymore.

My husband was now on the war path. Soon after the disastrous contact centre meeting, a different social worker came to interview me because "someone" had made an allegation to them that I was abusing the children. He said that he had found no evidence and could confirm – the "someone" was my husband. Then I was questioned under caution by the police, because "someone" had made an allegation to them that I was abusing the children. No further action was taken due to no evidence. The police officer said they could see it was my husband's revengeful ways.

We had to get a court order to ensure my safety when returning to our matrimonial home to get some of our clothes and belongings. I had a police escort to do this.

Protecting my children; my most precious gift

The following month brought about the most disastrous day for the children and me. It was the second Family Court hearing. This was an important one and my solicitor said I had to pay for a barrister. (I just missed out on Legal Aid, but my husband claimed he wasn't working and so used the system to his full advantage.) The room was also more imposing. The judge (in a normal suit) sat separately, we sat on benches and tables with our barristers and, when we gave evidence, we had to go to a lectern and swear on the Bible to tell the truth. This was a farce for my husband, who totally thought the Bible was false any way! It gave him free reign to lie as much as he wanted.

Sadly, my solicitor completely let us down and the whole case was a shambles. I was badly misrepresented - none of my witnesses were called, the report from the Domestic Violence team hadn't been submitted and my solicitor hadn't prepared my court papers correctly. So my barrister kept turning to me and saying "give me something" because he had nothing he could use to fight my husband's scurrilous accusations. In fact, my barrister sat with his head in his hands for most of the court hearing.

The Judge knew of the Social Services concerns but dismissed them. He even knew a report from Children and Family Court Advisory and Support Service (CAFCASS) was needed, but still granted my husband unsupervised contact! His barrister said I was a "witch, drunkard and a liar" and it was me who abused the children! The "witch" was because apparently I did spells – they were my prayers; the "drunkard" was because I had a sherry on a Sunday and the "liar" was because I had no evidence in the court bundle to prove I was telling the truth. The judge allowed it all and when my barrister tried to disallow the comments he had nothing to back it up with. The neighbours, who had seen the 'coleslaw' incident, lied on oath against me and the children. They said that the children had never told them that their daddy hurt them. In fact, the children had. The judge's ending comment was:

"This is a man of good character".

I ran out of the courtroom and fell, foetal position, in a corner. My niece, who had come with me, came over and tried to haul me up. She did not want my husband to see me and get some sick satisfaction from my misery. A court security guard rushed over and carried me to a private room. My niece took my face in her hands and sternly declared:

"We will fight this!"

We made sure he had left the building and then drove to the solicitors. I was struck dumb by the whole experience, but my niece tore an absolute strip off her and demanded to know what had gone wrong. The solicitor's patronising response astounded both of us:

"Tell the children not to worry and it will be alright."

It was then that we knew we had to get someone else to fight our case.

The children were totally distraught when we told them. I reassured them that they would not have to go. "If needs be we will run away and live in the car for a while." I meant it! I was in a no-win situation, as a judge had ordered unsupervised contact, but when I told the social worker what had happened, he said that if I adhered to that order, he would question my ability to keep the children safe and might actually put them in an interim foster home! That night, I can honestly say I sweated fear for the dear children. I slept on their bedroom floor. When I say slept, sleep did not come!

I had called the Women's Aid phone number I found online at 10pm that night. It was reassuring to hear a calm voice. She listened to me pour out what had happened; my care worker would be in touch early in the morning. She was, and she helped fight the following battles by coordinating all involved. Such a source of wisdom and care!

My lovely niece had been in touch with her solicitor friend that night and had a contact number for a solicitor that she had recommended. I rang the new solicitor the next morning and got an appointment to see her that same day. I told her our story and immediately she put in for an emergency court hearing. This was a Friday. She contacted the school and Social Services.

The problem we had though, was that my old (failed) solicitor still had all my papers and she had done some work, apparently, on my divorce and so wanted paying before she released anything. Shame on her! It was thousands of pounds and I certainly didn't have that kind of money but my dear nephew stepped forward and paid the bill. The money was from his house deposit that he had been saving up for years! My family had helped change the course of this battle.

"It's all been a misunderstanding"

We got into court the following Monday to appeal the unsupervised contact. It was a short half hour one, where we presented evidence from the social worker – my husband had exerted undue pressure on the children; he didn't want to help pay for them; his threats of suicide and, most importantly, the children were now thriving and their nightmares and bedwetting had stopped. The judge granted us a re-hearing, saying it was a "legal mess". My husband was there with his solicitor and was furious, especially as he should have been picking up the children from school that day. I quickly rang the children's school to tell them that under no circumstances was the children's dad allowed to take them. If only he could have been trusted and behaved decently, he would have got his wish.

When I collected the children that day, we firstly had a big celebratory family hug, and then I had a word with the head teacher. I thanked her for the notes that explained how the children would cry if their dad came to pick them up. They had been submitted to the court. I asked why she had never given me this information. Her answer was that "it was confidential and only shared on a need-to-know basis". I asked her to reconsider this stance as it could cause the perpetrator of a crime to go unpunished if information wasn't shared with all concerned to keep children safe.

(I must say here, that procedures have very much changed in education now and it is expected that all agencies who work with children share their information and have a duty of care to families.)

With a change of solicitor, we went back into court to get the decision of unsupervised contact over turned and for a further hearing for a 'Finding of Fact'. This is a court document that states the abuse that has occurred and the judge, after looking at the evidence, will (or will not) find them as fact. This is imperative to get the details right, as all following court cases use this. Eventually we won, after six court hearings, and the children were legally placed within my custody and residence. My husband was only allowed Supervised Contact.

As you can imagine, my husband was seething. He got a new solicitor and took me back to court saying that I was preventing him from seeing the children and he was also seeking that the Finding of Fact be dismissed. The truth was that he hadn't even tried to see them as he was ordered and told lies to the new solicitor. When we were in the Family Court room, the judge pointed out the home truths and the Finding of Fact document. This made the new solicitor look very foolish. My husband cannot bear anyone having authority over him and actually said to the judge,

"No F---er will tell me when I can see my own kids!"

At this point the Judge told him to start facing up to the reality that these were "Findings of Fact, not Findings of Accusations". The judge then told my husband that his actions in the room were showing that further investigation into his behaviour was needed and that he could not see the children at all, pending the completion of a CAFCASS report. He was only allowed indirect contact by letter. The CAFCASS report recommending no contact at all! This showed how dangerous the children's dad was (and still is!).

That same day I was told that my husband had put all the children's toys for sale on Gumtree. In fact throughout this time he showed he wasn't capable of meeting their needs – he never showed remorse, he denied any abuse, would only see the children on his terms (so he didn't see them), hindered me from getting their belongings, wouldn't pay maintenance and damaged their home.

My husband, through two more different solicitors, kept issuing more court proceedings, saying I was not allowing him to see his children. He never took up the offer of seeing them through the contact centre. The judge then stopped all contact as his letters were very emotionally abusing and his behaviour was showing he had no intention of admitting the harm he had done to us. I got well versed with the different parts of the Children's Act that were used to keep the children safe. My husband, through the court system, even insisted that I was psychologically assessed for depression and other harmful behaviour. The judge allowed a psychologist my husband had chosen, but said if I was to be assessed, then, he and the children should be too! It totally backfired on him, because the report clearly stated that it was him who had the behavioural issues and the children and I had suffered with depression. It explained that it was 'reactive depression' caused by his abuse!

The court hearings did eventually come to an end though – five years after the rescue. The judge put a ban on my husband taking me back to court again until the children were sixteen.

"Then they can vote with their feet if they want to see him." They never have.

If we had seen him, our feet would have run in the opposite direction; firstly because we still feared him and secondly I feared he would report me to the police for harassing him! It was his clever mind game to keep control over us. I will say, at the writing of this book, the fear has gone. We can see the sad reality of the man he is.

You could say this was all about protecting the physical wellbeing of the children, but what about their hearts, minds and souls? This is where the NSPCC come in. The children learned to find their voice and inner resolve through counselling, workshops and even campaigning for change to government policy. One of the children went to Parliament in London with a member of the NSPCC and met the Education Secretary. They discussed changes that needed to be made in the court system. Two of the required changes actually became law.

The first time I noticed their inner strength growing was the first Father's Day after our rescue. They didn't want to send their dad a card, but sent one to the old man who lived next door to our rented house!

They had always had an inner beauty. Even now, as I write this, I am so proud of their caring natures and how they make special occasions so precious with home-made cards and thoughtful days out. They spoil me with quite extravagant presents, which I don't feel I deserve, but they say I do... and more. Bless their hearts. We went to church for the first time in years on the Easter Sunday after our rescue and joined a congregation who were generous with their time and love. It was a place for us to belong and flourish. They were a mighty blessing through the stress of the court cases and threats instigated by my husband to disrupt our lives.

Through these experiences I learned to:

- Get a massive amount of evidence from everywhere you can think of, make sure it is in your court bundles.
- Make notes in a notebook about everything happening – recording dates, times and what was said and by whom. Especially noting if you need to respond to something. This is vital in combatting lies and shoddy professionals.
- Explain to your friends and family why life has become like it has; you will probably have been isolated from them by your abuser. I found honesty and making myself vulnerable with people I knew I could trust, enabled situations to become better than we ever thought. You will know who your friends are. I learned the ones who went against us were the ones who were never interested in how the children or myself were, they just told me "your husband is hurting so much, stop being so horrid to him, stop breaking up the marriage and allow him to see the children".
- Expect your abuser to lie. Don't be surprised, it's their mother-tongue.
- Compartmentalise the court system and all the horribleness away from normal life. The children and I

went to school and had a lovely home life as much as we were able. We had picnics and barbeques in the back garden. We went on walks in the woods and by the seaside. We made dens and played. We danced and we sang. We stored up those happy memories so they outweighed the bad.

- Try as much as you can to stop thoughts about the abuser, so they don't come into your new home and disrupt that as well. And especially do not think about them while in bed, it's like them being there with you….and you certainly don't want that!
- Ask for guidance from your solicitor, IDAS or NSPCC about the Children's Act to help fight your case. It may seem daunting. Please see the Glossary section at the back of this book for the parts of the Children's Act I used. If you have a computer, familiarise yourself or go to the library. Information is power!

Lastly, but most importantly, I will mention our heroes during this period:

- There was one particular solicitor and one particular district judge who had the authority, the law and the compassion to keep my children safe.
- The two people who dedicated their whole lives, for five years, to help fight against the incessant harassment and abuse from my husband, were my sister and her husband. They spent hours and days helping me write letters, prepare for court hearings, suffered harassment and false

accusations from my husband. They went through hell with us. My sister even came to every court hearing with me until my husband spat at her in the waiting room! We are eternally in debt to them for their unfailing love and support.

Because my husband got Legal Aid, he used it to his full advantage. There were twenty six court hearings in total! This cost me £56,000 in legal fees which came out of the proceeds of the house sale, when it was eventually sold. Our solicitor kept faith with me and waited to be paid for three years! I would have gladly paid ten times as much, if I had to, as the children really are my most precious gift.

- - - - -

When I had no words to express my helplessness, many of the psalms in the Bible supported me. Here is an abridged version of one that helped me through these times.

Psalm 73

"²But I had nearly lost confidence; my faith was almost gone ³because I was jealous of the proud when I saw that things go well for the wicked...
⁶And so they wear pride like a necklace and violence like a robe; ⁷their hearts pour out evil, and their minds are busy with wicked schemes.
⁸They laugh at other people and speak of evil things; they are proud and make plans to oppress others.
⁹They speak evil of God in heaven and give arrogant orders to everyone on earth...
¹³'Is it for nothing, then, that I have kept myself pure and have not committed sin?'...
¹⁶I tried to think this problem through, but it was too difficult for me
¹⁷until I went into God's Sanctuary. Then I understood what will happen to the wicked.
¹⁸You will put them in slippery places and make them fall to destruction! ...
²⁴You guide me with your instruction and at the end You will receive me with honour....
²⁶My mind and my body may grow weak, but God is my strength; He is all I ever need....
²⁸But as for me, how wonderful to be near God, to find protection with the Sovereign Lord and to proclaim all that He has done!"

The bit in bold highlights the fact – that if we concentrate only on the bad, that is all we will see. However, if you look for the good – you will find it!

A prayer:

Almighty God, thank You for all those family, friends and professionals that are there to support and fight for us. Please give strength and tenacity to all those who are fighting similar battles right now; encourage them to get the professional help they need.

Amen

11   When I thought it couldn't get worse!

I am being led into the Crown Court room, when I fall to my knees gasping for air. I am having a panic attack! I ask the young clerk to give me a minute as my Witness Support man wasn't with me and I needed a moment to compose myself. Her reply was, "Come on, get up, you don't want to make this judge angry."

<u>Crown Court for my husband's cruelty and neglect of the children</u>

The prosecution of my husband for the cruelty towards his children was a fiasco from start to finish.

After we were rescued, despite the:

- Social worker and CAFCASS reports,
- Financial compensation given to the children by the Criminal Injuries Compensation Authority (CICA) acknowledging the evidence of the physical and emotional abuse they had suffered at the hands of their dad

...the police said it was his word against mine.

It actually took the Police Child Protection Unit until a year and two months after the rescue to interview the children about what they had suffered at the hands and mouth of their dad. Under the advice of the Police, I never talked through the events we had suffered because I didn't want anyone to say that I had imprinted a false memory in the children's minds. That approach backfired.

As months were going by and the legal procedures were not progressing, I could see the children were really struggling and needed emotional support. So I sought the help of the NSPCC and the children received magnificent counselling. The Crown Court hearing happened three years after we were rescued and by that time the children had 'buried' some of the events.

When the time was approaching for the four-day hearing, the children, our witnesses and I all went to the Court House and were shown around by a man from Witness Support. He gave advice about speaking clearly to the jury, the judge would be in a red gown with wearing a wig and that we should not let the defence team provoke us. He said he would be with us every step of the way. We all agreed that it felt better that we now knew what would be happening.

On day one of the hearing, I was the first into the witness box, as I was the applicant (prosecution) and they always go first. He was the respondent (defence) and so went when all our evidence had been shown. When I entered the Crown Court room, I looked a mess. I was slightly staggering because of my panic attack and trying to calm my breathing. It was about five minutes into the hearing that my Witness Support man came in. I thought, "you are too late, I am already 'a lamb to the slaughter' and you were not there when I needed you". He told me later that he'd received a phone call and hadn't realised our case had been called.

When I thought it couldn't get worse!

My experience of the Criminal Justice System shocked me. It did not achieve justice for our family and could have easily destroyed us. For example:

- It took three years to come to trial. My local MP was so astonished by the shambolic handling by Crown Prosecution Service (CPS) and the police that he wrote to them demanding answers. The police authority eventually apologised for the mishandling of the case.

- My barrister took only ten minutes before the hearing to talk to me. She was cold and officious. I felt I couldn't ask any questions. When we were in the hearing, she never tried to put me at ease. When I was being bullied by the defence team and clearly struggling, she never interjected or tried to step in to defend me.

- At the time, I tried not to worry too much because I thought the professional witnesses would be on stand, plus the photographic evidence the police had taken of the damage done to the house showed what my husband was capable of - 'the man behind closed doors'. In fact, the witnesses were not called and the photographic evidence was not shown.

- In my husband's second statement for the Family Court he had written "I did have a knife, but I never intended to use it." In court the barrister twisted his words and said it was the knife he was eating with that he had just wafted in the air. In fact, my husband had told the children to get the carving knife from the drawer and said:

    "If you lie you'll lose your tongue."

- The Judge told the jury early on in the trial that "this man will not go to prison".

- The children had to attend the same court building as their dad and were put in a little room with a television in it. They were individually televised into the court room. No one was there to help them understand the barrister's questions. My husband's barrister was maliciously dogged towards the children and refused to let them answer correctly. She painted the picture she wanted the jury to hear. The children were toddlers when their dad started to hurt them but my husband's barrister pressed them for dates of their abuse. They were sobbing all alone in a room and no one showed any compassion, not even my barrister. It was a horrific experience!

- The judge paraphrased what one of the children had said completely incorrectly.

- The police officer in charge of our case for three years was only on stand for five minutes. When she came out she was apoplectic with frustration and said:

  "What the f--- was that about?"

- None of our professional witnesses were called to repeat what the children had said to them or vouch that they were of good character and known for telling the truth.

- The hearing finished a day early and my Witness Support man rang to say he had been found not guilty because there was "an element of doubt". (In Crown Court hearings, decisions are made on a 'beyond all reasonable doubt' basis whereas, in Family Court, decisions are made 'on a balance of probabilities'.)

I was told I could appeal but I had promised the children that they would never have to go on the stand again. I couldn't break that promise and, despite my own emotions, put their feelings and wellbeing first, knowing full well that my husband would use this verdict and prolong his campaign to ridicule, harass and discredit me. True to form he did his very best but the ridicule I had feared from the people around us was insignificant when compared with the sympathy and support provided by most people. No one could believe the total injustice our family had suffered.

- - - - -

It was the Easter Holidays. Straight after the trial I took the children to London. We found a Travelodge for dinner, bed and breakfast - £40 for all of us! We got train tickets through the local paper - £10 each return - and the museums were all free.

We had such an absorbing time. When we got back to school the children just spoke about their amazing adventure in London and not the disastrous court hearing.

However, once we got settled back into school, my husband used this victory to his full advantage and caused mischief at my work and with everyone we knew – family and friends. I feared I would lose my job, the children and my reputation.

"It's all been a misunderstanding"

I rang the Samaritans. I was in utter torment. The Crown Court debacle was worse than the abuse.

My husband thought he was being clever after the Crown Court hearing, by using the same barrister that represented him there to start more Family Court proceedings against me. However, she was made to feel foolish as my husband hadn't given her all the documentation. This made me wonder what documentary evidence had actually been submitted in the Crown Court bundle. There were at least eleven pieces of evidence in my statement to the Child Protection Unit. I had assumed they had been submitted for my Crown Court bundle. The Family Court judge virtually growled at the barrister saying:

> "How dare you come into my court room and tell me my judgements are wrong."

It felt like a small victory.

The children also suffered flash backs about their abuse and the nightmares and bedwetting started again. One of the children would start hyperventilating and want to damage things. They didn't. The other said they wanted to stab their dad. My response was:

> "Children we are going to live the best lives possible. You are going to grow to be the most decent human beings and that will be the biggest 'up yours' to him, as he grows to be a bitter lonely old man!"

When I thought it couldn't get worse!

Our anger and frustration was palpable. Thank the Lord, the NSPCC helped us vent these feelings; acknowledged them as real, and then worked out a way forward so we could leave it all behind. I had started pulling at my hair, hitting and biting myself; something I hadn't done since the rescue. The support of Woman's Aid and IDAS helped me overcome this.

I struggled to understand why my husband didn't get convicted until, two years after the Crown Court trial, God spoke to me in a dream and said:

"If he had gone to prison, as he should have, he would have pretended to be reformed, been released and would have been back into your lives again. He would have caused havoc, the children would be mentally messed up and you would be in a hospital for the mentally ill."

Legal justice in the court was denied to us but, much more importantly, since then, we have lived without him gloriously.

The lessons from this stage of the journey include to:

- Know you have power. Don't let the barrister make you feel like they have all the power.
- Ask to see what is in the court bundle. If things aren't in that should be, make sure they are put in.
- Check which witnesses are coming and insist they come if they haven't been called.
- Take a deep breath and take time answering when in the witness box; you only have one chance so take it.

"It's all been a misunderstanding"

- Make sure you get the truth across; expect it to be twisted.
- Tell yourself that you are a person of worth – God's creation - and try your utmost not to be provoked into emotional outbursts.

- - - - -

My friend sent me a text after my husband was found not guilty:

"Therefore put on the full armour of God, so that when the day of evil comes, you may be able to stand your ground, and after you have done everything, to stand." (Ephesians Chapter 6 Verse 13)

The truth will out! I try my best to stand tall!

A prayer:

Dear Jesus, when dark days come, You can show us how to fight back with the words and promises of the Bible. Thank You for the transformation that can come when we trust in You. Please be close to those who are at the end of themselves and speak words of reassurance to their inner being.

Amen

12 It's not just people that hurt you; systems and red tape do too

Compensation - For the failings of my first solicitor

"Just tell the children not to worry and it will be all right!"

That was the view of my first solicitor after the initial Family Court judge had granted my husband unconditional access to the children.

This compensation matter was about getting the thousands of pounds we paid back from the first solicitor who failed us in the divorce and children related matters. We also sought compensation for all the anxiety it had caused and the legal costs we'd incurred to put our case back on track again.

My new firm of solicitors provided a different person for each of my cases - one for the children, one for the divorce, one for the house conveyance and one for helping me fight the criminal allegations my husband had made against me. The firm made quite a joke about it all, and said it was like I was playing a game of "legal bingo"!

When I used a solicitor from the same firm for my compensation claim, I had expected the same level of tenacity, as the rest of their solicitors had shown me. I know you shouldn't judge someone by their handshake, but when we shook hands for the first time my heart sank! It was weak and he just shook the tips of my fingers!

In a nutshell, over the next three years the old solicitor's legal department didn't take our plight seriously and kept denying there was a claim! Even when presented with the evidence that the solicitor had failed to tell my witnesses there was a court hearing they needed to attend! They dismissed all of our letters with no thought as to how it was affecting our family. Even the lady from IDAS was shocked at their attitude, especially as they were a Family Law firm. However, my solicitor just didn't have the strong-minded determination needed to fight back.

The tide turned after a conversation with a church friend who was a barrister at the time.

She was a proper 'knight in shining armour'! In her own time, for hours and hours, she poured over my court bundles and found the legal flaws where the old solicitor had failed. She made all the legal arguments my solicitor should have done and presented a lock tight case of failings that the old solicitor couldn't deny.

It took another three years, but the old firm did eventually admit they'd got it wrong. They settled (quite substantially) out of court, as I was going to go to the papers to shame them! How dare they treat human beings like that and hide behind red tape?! They are meant to be a firm that helps families, not makes them suffer. Thank God for my dear barrister friend, without her, we wouldn't have had victory.

It's not just people that hurt you; systems and red tape do too

Compensation - Criminal Injuries Compensation Authority (CICA)

"How stupid is that Chairwoman, did she actually read your file?"

The Victim Support man was fuming and as flabbergasted as I was. We were in the waiting room after hearing her judgement. I was so furious I was having palpitations. In fact, as I write now I can feel my ire burning within me.

The children had been given compensation by CICA, for the abuse they had suffered from their dad, years before. (They received £1,000 each.)

Now I was in a tribunal for my compensation hearing with a new Victim Support man. After I had been interviewed, referring to the 'coleslaw' incident, the Chairwoman said that I had deserved the slap my husband had given me, because I had slapped him first! She concluded that I was not eligible for compensation from the scheme.

Her words hit me like another hand slapping me. It was like I was in the room with my ex-husband again. She was telling me that I deserved to be slapped!

I was shaking and holding back my tears. I protested; there were statements from the police and social workers and Finding of Fact documents in my file to corroborate my evidence.

The Victim Support man, who was supposed to just sit by my side as a silent moral support, broke protocol. He asked the Chairwoman if she had actually read the whole of my file and pointed out that the 'coleslaw' incident was a one-off after years of bullying and intimidation from my husband.

She insisted her decision to deny compensation was right.

I was worn out and thought I would just let it go. It was a battle I wasn't going to win. The Victim Support man urged me to appeal gave me the details of the Appeals Court in London and said he was going to get a transcript of the hearing.

On receiving the transcript of the hearing, I took a deep breath and prayed for authority over the case. It took me four long days to compose my eight-page response, highlighting every word and paragraph where she had got things wrong.

The Upper Appeal Court in London granted me an appeal.

My Victim Support man was so proud of me. He said he'd never had someone like me willing to challenge a Tribunal Chairperson's decision. I said the appeal being granted was an answer to prayer.

There was a wait of another year before the Appeal Tribunal meeting took place.

When we entered the waiting room, I was surprised to see two of the lovely police officers who had helped the children and me. We smiled and did a quick nod of our heads to each other. No one said anything. Then we were all asked to go into the tribunal room. It was just like a family court room. The police officers sat behind us.

After the Chairman introduced himself, he asked me to explain what had happened to me. I did it as succinctly as I could. Then he asked the officers if what I had said was true. They said yes. The judge then tipped his head to one side and looked at me for some time with compassion:

"You just want to be heard, don't you?"

Tears rolled down my face.

"Yes."

I realised the tissue I was holding had been twisted and twisted as I had been wringing my hands. He then apologised for the lack of justice I had received in this process and awarded me my £1,000 compensation! As for the Chairwoman, I was told she had been sent for retraining!

I just wanted to rush out of my chair and hug everyone! I was in a room full of men and they had all been wonderful to me and my children. However, I contained myself. I said I was very grateful and thankful to each and every one of them in a contained poised way.

It was when the Victim Support man and I were in the car park alone that we jumped for joy and danced and hugged each other. Six years and seven months after our rescue, this was the end of my court and tribunal cases.

Even though money was tight, I used quite a lot of it for going on an adventure holiday with the children, some for an oven that worked and the rest for a new computer for us all. We felt great!

What I learned:

- Justice is always worth fighting for.
- Go with your gut instinct, if things feel wrong, they probably are. There is a saying: 'if in doubt – out'. Don't accept shoddy professionals – you are paying for a service.
- Always be respectful and as rational as possible.
- Always get help from volunteer support services like Victim Support and IDAS. Don't try and do it all on your own. Their advice is free and they came to my hearings and gave invaluable advice and care.
- Ask for a transcript of the hearing if things go wrong. This is a very valid tool for all court hearings. You have the right to ask for them; then you can examine the details of the papers and challenge the errors in writing.

- - - - -

It's not just people that hurt you; systems and red tape do too

There is a book in the Bible called Romans and in Chapter twelve, it says:

"¹²Be joyful in hope, patient in affliction and faithful in prayer. ¹⁷Do not repay anyone evil for evil. Be careful to do what is right in the eyes of everyone. ¹⁸If it is possible, as far as it depends on you, live at peace with everyone. ¹⁹Do not take revenge, my dear friends, but leave room for God's wrath, for it is written: 'It is mine to avenge; I will repay,' says the Lord. ²¹Do not be overcome by evil, but overcome evil with good."

A prayer:

Dear Jesus, when life is really hard and some of it doesn't make sense, please take away the burden of getting revenge so I can move on and flourish in Your new life! Please raise up a people of integrity within the legal system and thank You for all faithful carriers of justice.

Amen

13   This is a reason, but not an excuse

I'm staring at some letters headed 'Child Support Agency' and in exasperation cry out:

"Why can't he just behave decently?"

Money Matters

When I wrote in the last chapter that the court and tribunal struggles were at an end, I had one last thorn in my side....Child Maintenance. At the point of this book being published, despite the children now being in their twenties, my ex-husband cannot let his campaign of control and hate come to an end and will not pay the final £5,500 he has owed us for years! My local MP is helping with this.

Clearly the majority of 'non-resident' parents are decent people trying their best to provide financial support for their children. I wonder what it is that makes some think it's ok not to pay maintenance.

My husband had done everything not to pay, such as falsifying his earnings, declaring only £5,000 for his self-employment income to the Tax Man and becoming a student. The Experian alerts I got showed he was using our joint names to get numerous loans. I 'dissociated' myself from him on my Credit File. He also made sure the house was repossessed by the building society so I had to wait for a court order for money to be released to me. His incessant applications to the Family Court were a financial drain, and he used the Legal Aid system to get all his legal fees paid for!

One thing that did work in our favour was Child Tax Credits. He must have been so annoyed when they started being paid directly to me and what a difference they made to our daily lives. He was also made to pay back the money he had fraudulently obtained for claiming one of our children was disabled.

The Child Maintenance Service (CMS), as it is called now, did everything within their power to get money for the children, including hiring a private detective. The key to success with the CMS was getting my local MP involved; when he became involved, the money began to arrive. I came to see Child Maintenance as a saving scheme. We lived day-by-day within our limited means (as he would not pay anything for months) then a lump sum would arrive which would enable me to do something special for the children.

Sometimes these delayed maintenance payments were a lot of money. On one occasion we enjoyed a longboat holiday on the Norfolk Broads, on another an adventure holiday with a motorhome and one time we had three weeks in Canada!

- - - - -

I don't believe my ex-husband was born with an aggressive, manipulative nature, but things must have happened to him that moulded his behaviour and character into something that was controlling and frightening. There were marks on his back that looked like whip marks. He lied so much that I think lying had become his mother-tongue. He couldn't tell the truth or recognise it even when presented with clear facts.

There was one other element that didn't help our situation; he started to take some kind of drug in the last two years we were together. This could have been a reason why he became more erratic and menacing. I asked him to seek help, I forgave him and we did stay – until it became too dangerous.

In the end, his consuming fear of losing his family and his status in the community was a principal cause of exactly that; he lost them both. He created what he feared most.

So the children's dad may have had some reasons why he abused us, but it doesn't excuse his rotten behaviour.

Things I learned:

- Remember to write down every phone call and letter you have received from anyone connected with your case. This is essential evidence in convincing the authorities of the danger of your circumstances and important in making your case for protection and maintenance.
- Make sure you make full use of the help of voluntary support systems like IDAS and Citizen's Advice Bureau. The CMS letters are formatted to be used in many scenarios so if you don't understand what they are saying, ring them or set up an online account and get advice.

- If Witness Support isn't available to support you in a tribunal, take a level-headed friend. My friend helped me keep calm when my ex-husband was saying his money transfers were all legal. No judge likes it if the people in front of them are making faces or 'huffing'. When I started getting agitated she gently kicked me under the table! This was a good reminder to compose myself and just keep taking the notes.
- Get your local MP involved as soon as the CMS fail to carry out what their letters say they are going to do.
- If the CMS say your case is a "complex" one, it basically means that the child's non-resident parent is self-employed or a director of a firm. Be prepared for a struggle!
- Do not over analyse your ex-partner's behaviour, they are probably suffering too, but do not allow yourself to go back into a dangerous situation. They need help just as much as you do, but until they can maintain a change in behaviour they cannot be trusted.
- It is important to know what is in your credit file and also to dissociate yourself from your former partner.

- - - - -

"It's all been a misunderstanding"

This Bible verse helped to keep me grounded, and not become greedy in my fight to get money for the children.

"Keep your lives free from the love of money, and be satisfied with what you have. For God has said, 'I will never leave you; I will never abandon you.' Let us be bold, then, and say, 'The Lord is my helper, I will not be afraid. What can anyone do to me?' "
(Hebrews Chapter 13 Verses 5 and 6)

A prayer:

God grant me the serenity to accept the things I cannot change; the courage to change the things I can; and wisdom to know the difference.

Amen

14   Things like this don't happen to people like me

My aim in writing this book is to give hope to those who have experienced or are experiencing domestic violence or abusive relationships.

It is written for those who have faith in God and for those who do not.

I am a Christian and while that didn't protect me or my children from harm, I always knew Jesus was my source of inner strength and comfort throughout it all.

This chapter is an example of how He is so much more than just a friend.

'Blessedly bendy'!

This event happened when I was at an annual Christian summer camp for teenagers, about 27,000 people were there! The camp has everything that a teenager could possibly want to keep happy and active. I take a group every year from our church.

This particular year, our group had eighteen teenagers (including my children) and five adults. With the help of a friend I was doing the catering for the group. It's an awesome time to see God working in these youngsters. I was looking forward to the event but I was crippled with my back pain.

Thirty years previously, I had done a parachute jump for Mencap and landed badly. In those days you practiced one day and the next, you would jump out of the plane on your own! I had injuries in my feet, knees and back. A few months before the camp I had just had an operation to correct the worsening damage to my knee. I was in extreme pain with my back. This was because some of the joints in my lower back had fused together (arthritis) and one part of my spinal column had actually worn away to look like a wedge of cheese. This caused terrible sciatic pains to shoot down my legs, arms and fingers.

My future was looking bleak so the doctor recommended injections and a cage fitted to my lower back. Even though the cage was daunting at least it was going to help stabilise my back. I was unable to bend, sneeze, sleep or walk without excruciating pain. Unfortunately the cage isn't on the NHS! So my long-term prognosis was very depressing. To make matters worse, I'd been to a chiropractor in the hope he would help me, but he had made it much worse. He had caused my spine to be twisted. I was 'under exercise' on prescription to help make it better.

At the camp, we have to sit on the floor for the Big Tent worship sessions and this was impossible for me so I had to sit on a chair away from my group. By the second night I was in such agony and in a bad way that I went to the doctors on site. They gave me painkillers, said a prayer over me and allowed me to sleep in a darkened room for a bit. I delegated the cooking the next day and the group were wonderful. We were all very concerned though, especially my children.

The week went by very quickly and God had moved amazingly among us and the worship and teaching and sense of community were so restoring. The miracles of healing in mind, body and soul were astounding but I was still in immense pain. However, on the last night a chap called Robby Dawkins spoke and when he'd finished he invited all those suffering with back pain to come forward. He was quite specific about the back pain and he described my symptoms down to the very last detail. All would be prayed over but only those with the mentioned pains were invited to go to the side stage area.

My friend, very firmly told me to go forward as I was refusing to at first. Things like miracles don't happen to people like me but I took a deep breath and went up. (I will point out that the last night at the camp always has a theme and this year it was onesies – what a sight we were!) Robby showed us a way to pray for healing and how we were to pray for each other. So, one of my group came forward and started to pray the way we had been shown, then a lady from the camp choir came and sang the most beautiful songs over me. She also said, "do not fear". I said to Jesus that if He was willing then please heal me now! In fact, I was most irreverent, and actually said, "If you are going to do it – DO IT!" I held my arms out in front of me.

As I was standing, I was peaceful and then I felt another hand touch my arm so I opened my eyes. It was a young lad of about twenty; with sever cerebral palsy, in front of me. It is against the rules for mixed gender praying (for safeguarding reasons) but he did have a lanyard with "Staff" on it, so I knew he worked for the camp. I just thought I'd go with it as Jesus didn't always follow rules!

I felt myself swaying and was aware of a warm pressure at my back. It was gentle and I just went with it, as I felt safe. I have no idea how much time passed but I felt it time to open my eyes. It was then that I became aware that I was on the floor and looking at legs!

I must admit that my first reaction was that of embarrassment and jumped quickly off the floor. Then it suddenly dawned on me how easily I got up, usually I have to go on all fours then carefully push up with my hands moving up my legs. (Just writing this brings tears of gratitude to God.) So I quickly dropped down flat on the floor again because I thought it was a fluke! But…. I got up as easily as I did the first time! Very irreverently, again, I shouted, "Bloody hell!" Oh my goodness, we were all shouting and screaming praises to God. I realised that two others from my group had come across and they were now in tears. I was told that as the prayers were being said I was moving my hips as if I was doing an invisible hoola hoop! What a sight! That caused many to smile. I was now able to bend and move pain-free.

Fantastic as this was and is, the next part will blow your mind!

I found out that the young lad, that had come to pray over me, was called David and he was ecstatic. He was screaming and he kept using sign language to tell me something, but I didn't understand. He made motions that I thought he was saying he wanted a photo and he pointed to the sky and I thought he was saying – "thank you God". He kept shaking his head so we went to one of the sign language people at the camp and David did the same actions. Then he was getting a bit cross with the lady and kept shaking his head. So the lady took a deep breath, turned to me and told me what David was hand-signing. She thought it didn't make sense and had just literally interpreted what David signed. I kid you not, when she told me what he'd signed to her I nearly got knocked off my feet again!

David had hand-signed that, when I walked by him to go to the stage, he got a picture in his mind's eye of me ....falling out of an aeroplane!!! I gasped.

It's so astounding that I still shake my head. So I told David and the lady that he was right and I'd done a parachute jump 30 years ago and had landed badly and was in a terrible degenerative state because of it. But my back was now flexible and pain-free. Then it dawned on me … I had done the parachute jump for Mencap!!!! I looked at David and shrieked "I did it for you!"

Do you know, I just couldn't make it up! God has an amazing sense of humour! My children and I then found each other and hugged each other in a tearful, shocked huddle. They really still don't know what to make of it.

I woke the following morning still bendy and a massive smile on my face. By the end of the day we had packed up camp, travelled home in a coach for six hours and unpacked our tent at home and I was still pain-free. (Well, apart from the tops of my legs as I was so excited that I kept doing lunges, as I've not been able to do any for years!)

So I went to the doctors to see what had happened. I didn't tell him about the miracle at first and asked him to measure me. (In the past year I had lost 3cm from my height.) He didn't understand why he had to do it as he'd only measured me about two weeks previously. I just asked again. So as I stood against the wall and he measured me a look of puzzlement came over his face. He asked me to stand away from the wall again and then he measured me again. Then he looked at my feet to see if I had heels on – I didn't. So he slowly walked to his computer and noted that I'd grown a centimetre and a half! Wow! I then told him my miracle story. My doctor didn't know what to make of it and asked me what he should put on record – I told him to put BLESSEDLY BENDY!

And that is what I am.

The pain and clicking in my spine come sometimes, but I must not fear. I will keep trusting in our heavenly Father who loves us. I'm very aware that I must give glory to God and Jesus being our healer when I tell this story. May He use me for His glorious will to be done on earth.

And so I hope this story inspires you to go out of your comfort zone and ask in faith for healing. God sometimes does exactly as we ask straightaway and sometimes He's got something far better for us and we may just have to wait in His loving hands. The key to all of this is - trusting in His divine presence to get us through.

- - - - -

Things like this don't happen to people like me

Through all of this I remembered the Bible verse,

"Trust in the Lord with all your heart and never rely on what you think you know. Remember the Lord in everything you do and He will show you the right way." (Proverbs Chapter 3 Verses 5 and 6)

A prayer:

Dear Father God, thank You, that in the midst of our ordinary lives, You move wonderfully to change our lives in better ways than we could imagine. Please help us to live in expectancy of Your greatness and power.

Amen

Next steps - Healing

Our children deserve to be guided and supported into enriching relationships and environments. My passion now is to:

Continue helping change the court systems.

Go into schools and colleges and teach about positive relationships.

Encourage teaching professionals to speak up and share any concerns they have for children; they could save lives.

Highlight the need to learn to listen well to children.

"I know what it is to be in need, and I know what it is to have plenty. I have learned the secret of being content in any and every situation, whether well fed or hungry, whether living in plenty or in want. I can do all this through Him who gives me strength."

(Philippians Chapter 4 Verses 12 and 13)

15 And finally...

Please don't make the same mistakes I made.

If you are male or female and someone is hurting you, get help and get out!

Speak up. Don't assume people know what you are going through. SAY SOMETHING. At the children's school, I was subliminally begging them to notice our plight and bring us in and talk about the children's withdrawn behaviour. They didn't. I learned that it was up to me to speak out and then help comes.

Let forgiveness come in early. The word forgiveness has the word 'give' in it. That's a clue. We give the hurt and harm away (to God). Forgiveness doesn't minimise harm, nor does it accept the perpetrator's behaviour - they must experience the consequences of their actions - but it *can* free survivors from the effects of abuse. One survivor put it like this:

"Forgiveness can free us from carrying someone else's burden - someone else's shame - someone else's wickedness. That is for them to carry alone. And when it comes, when forgiveness shows up, it feels free and it brings life; abundant life. Yes, forgiveness feels impossible, but it's also like the most holy thing there is."

Forgiveness with justice is best for the whole of society.

And finally...

Be open to see that, although the justice you wanted may not have happened as you wanted it to, over time, something more meaningful may have occurred instead. Please don't miss out on feeling the joy that might be happening in your life right at that moment.

Remember you have talents and are of value and worth – a precious part of God's creation.

Bring good to the world around you, even when you are going through the abuse; it will lift your spirits and inner strength. I completely understand how your head space and physical exhaustion can take over sometimes. I had panic attacks, reactive depression, a stroke and I self-harmed. The children suffered horrendous emotional breakdowns. With help and support, you must try your best to lift yourself out of it as much as you can. It is worth it for the well-being and future of you and your children.

As I finish this book, I have come to realise that the title of this book isn't just about our abuser twisting a horrendous situation to meet his own needs and inadequacies; it is also about my own misunderstandings about God. I thought I had to stay to show God's love to my husband, in the hope he would come into a relationship with Jesus. I was wrong.

It is my hope that we all come to know what a positive relationship is, and through these, make this world as it should be – a place to flourish, do good and have fun!

- - - - -

"It's all been a misunderstanding"

Bible: Hebrews Chapter 10 Verses 35-36 and Chapter 11 verse 1

"So do not throw away your confidence; it will be richly rewarded. You need to persevere so that when you have done the will of God, you will receive what He has promised."

"Now faith is confidence in what we hope for and assurance about what we do not see."

My prayer for you:

Dear Lord, may all those who have read this book find it a source of hope. Please let it be helpful and inspire them to be brave, loving and resilient people; to Your glory.

Amen

The Paperwork Bit - Being Informed

I am enclosing this next section for you to use as a quick reference tool. It may help you through the legal processes.

Please don't be put off by the amount, take out the sections you need, rather than try and digest it all at once.

It's not a definitive list; you can use the internet, libraries and supporting agencies as well.

I was too afraid to use my phone or computer to seek help, because I knew my husband monitored these.

I should have gone to the library and used the computer there. I would have found support that way. You must do the same. Don't waste time!

Remember - information is power!

i. Glossary

Ancillary Relief Proceedings - The proceedings concerned with the financial matters are known as ancillary relief because the financial matters are seen as being ancillary to the divorce proceedings.

Barrister - Barristers are specialists in certain legal fields that solicitors can instruct on behalf of their client to appear in court.

CAFCASS (Children and Family Court Advisory and Support Service) - Cafcass usually get involved in child proceedings once you or your former partner has submitted an application to the court. The role of Cafcass is to safeguard and promote the welfare of children. The court usually asks Cafcass advisors to work with families and advise the family court of the interests, needs, wishes and feelings of a child.

Contact Order - A Contact Order is requiring the person with whom the child lives (regardless of whether there is a Residence Order in force or not) to allow the child to visit or stay with the person named in the Order.

Crown Court - a Crown Court is a court in which criminal cases are tried by a judge and jury rather than by a magistrate.

Dissociate – disconnect or separate (in connection with your credit file).

Glossary

Family Court/ County Court - a civil court of law that hears cases involving domestic issues such as divorce and child custody.

Finding of Fact Hearing – A court hearing where the court will make a decision as to whether alleged incidents did or did not happen. Evidence is heard, which will normally include parties being cross-examined. After having heard the evidence, the judge will decide whether the alleged incidents happened or not. Most commonly, these allegations concern domestic abuse. Domestic abuse includes neglect, emotional, sexual, financial and physical harm.

HMRC - Her Majesty's Revenue and Customs is responsible for the collection of taxes, the payment of some forms of state support and the administration of other regulatory regimes including the national minimum wage and the issuance of national insurance numbers.

Lawyer - The term 'lawyer' is an umbrella term for both solicitors and barristers.

Legal Aid - Legal Aid can help meet the costs of legal advice, family mediation and representation in a court or tribunal.

You'll usually need to show that:
- your case is eligible for legal aid
- the problem is serious
- you cannot afford to pay for legal costs

You could for example get legal aid if:
- you or your family are at risk of abuse or serious harm, for example domestic violence or forced marriage
- you're at risk of homelessness or losing your home

- you've been accused of a crime, face prison or detention
- you're being discriminated against
- you need family mediation
- you're adding legal arguments or bringing a case under the Human Rights Act

Magistrates Court - the lowest level of criminal court, which has some civil authority in family and licensing matters. All criminal cases will start here. A magistrate (a legal officer) imposes a penalty on those who are either found guilty or plead guilty to offences.

NFA – No Further Action. When police have been asked to conduct an investigation and no evidence is found to support any further action being taken.

Parental Responsibility - Under the Children Act 1989 Section 3 (1), "parental responsibility" means all the rights, duties, powers, responsibilities and authority which, by law, a parent of a child has in relation to the child and his property.

Residence and Contact Hearings - This happens in a Family Court, where a judge, after assessing the presented evidence, decides which parent the child/ren will live with and how often the non-**resident** parent should have **contact** with the child/ren.

Residence Order - A Residence Order is an order settling the arrangements to be made as to the person with whom the child is to live.

Solicitor - Solicitors provide general legal advice on a variety of issues.

Glossary

<u>Witness Support</u>- provide free and independent support for both prosecution and defence witnesses in every criminal court in England and Wales.

ii. Helplines

ii.1.   The Police

Call the UK police on 101, if you need support or advice from the police and it's not an emergency. If you're deaf or hard of hearing, use our textphone service on 18001 101. **If you are in immediate danger please call 999**

Dialling 999 If you find yourself in the situation of having to make a silent 999 call to police, you must listen carefully to the emergency operator and follow instructions given to you. This is the same for calls from a landline or mobile phone. However, please be aware that it is extremely difficult for the police to trace the location of mobile phone calls, so any indication you can give of your location, even if you have to whisper, is vital.

If you dial 999 but are unable to speak, keep the line open and listen carefully to what the emergency operator says.

At the start of the call they will ask: **"Emergency which service?"** If you do not respond they will then ask: **"Do you need Fire, Police or Ambulance?"**

If you still do not respond the operator will say: **"What number have you dialled please? I cannot release your line until you say that you do not need an emergency service"**

and then: **"If you are unable to speak but need an emergency service, please tap the handset, cough or make a noise"**.

If the operator does not get a response to any of the above questions but can hear background voices, they can connect the call to a system that asks you to **press "55"** on your keypad if you want the police.

Responding in one of the above ways will prompt the operator to quickly connect to the police.

ii.2. National and Local Support Agencies

ii.2.1. National Domestic Abuse Helpline

0808 2000 247 or www.nationaldahelpline.org.uk

ii.2.2. Women's Aid Domestic Violence Helpline

Free 24-hour national helpline run by Women's Aid and Refuge. Phone: 0808 2000 247 For an information and support service email at helpline@womensaid.org.uk or info@womensaid.org.uk. There is an opportunity for a live chat on the Women's Aid website - hours of opening are Monday to Friday 10am to 4pm, Saturday and Sunday 10am to 12pm. Also, there is a survivor's handbook to help with aspects of domestic abuse, such as women's housing, safety planning, dealing with police.

ii.2.3. The Hideout

Women's Aid have created this online safe space to help children and young people to understand domestic abuse, and how to take positive action if it's happening to you. Search thehideout.org.uk

ii.2.4. IDAS

The largest specialist charity in Yorkshire supporting people affected by domestic abuse and sexual violence. Their services include refuge accommodation, community based support, peer mentoring, group work and access to a free, confidential out of hours' helpline. Phone 03000 110 110 (North Yorkshire and Barnsley) or 0808 808 2241 (Sheffield)

ii.2.5. NSPCC (National Society for the Prevention of Cruelty to Children)

Help for adults concerned about a child. They provide therapeutic services to help children move on from abuse, as well as supporting parents and families in caring for their children. They help professionals make the best decisions for children and young people, and support communities to help prevent abuse from happening in the first place. Phone 0808 800 5000

ii.2.6. Childline

Help for children and young people who are struggling emotionally or in fear of abuse. Phone 0800 1111

ii.2.7. Domestic Violence Assist

Specialises in assistance to obtain emergency injunctions from being further abused. Phone: 0800 195 8699

ii.2.8. Hourglass

The Hourglass confidential helpline provides information and support to anyone concerned about harm, abuse or exploitation of an older person. Phone: 0808 808 8141

ii.2.9. Men's Advice Line

Confidential helpline for male victims of domestic abuse. Phone: 0808 801 0327

ii.2.10. National LGBT Domestic Abuse Helpline

Emotional and practical support for LGBT+ people. Phone: 0800 999 5428

ii.2.11. National Stalking Helpline

Guidance on the law, how to report stalking, gathering evidence, staying safe and reducing the risk. Phone: 0808 802 0300

ii.2.12. Victim Support

Free and confidential help to victims of crime, witnesses, their family and friends. Phone: 0808 1689 111

ii.2.13. Citizens Advice Witness Service

Provides free and independent support for both prosecution and defence witnesses in every criminal court in England and Wales. Trained volunteers provide practical information about the court process as well as emotional support to help witnesses feel more confident when giving evidence. (Online)

They can:
- provide information about the court process
- show witnesses the courtroom ahead of the trial
- be there to talk to in confidence
- accompany witnesses when they give their evidence
- be there to give support on the day of the trial; at verdict and sentencing
- help prepare witnesses who need extra support, this can be at their home or another safe place
- help claim expenses
- work with other agencies to make sure the right support is provided

- refer witnesses to our partners, including local Citizens Advice after the trial for support with other issues

ii.2.14. The Mix

Offer free information and support for under 25s in the UK. Phone 0808 808 4994

ii.2.15. Samaritans

A registered charity aimed at providing emotional support to anyone in emotional distress, struggling to cope, or at risk of suicide throughout the United Kingdom and Ireland, often through their telephone helpline. Phone 116 123 (24/7 service)

ii.2.16. Bright Sky Domestic Abuse App

Available in 4 languages: English, Urdu, Punjabi and Polish. A unique UK-wide directory of specialist domestic abuse support services with contact details. There is a secure My Journal tool to record incidents of abuse via text, audio, video or photo form, without any of the content being saved on the device itself. There are questionnaires to assess the safety of a relationship, plus a section on dispelling myths around domestic and sexual abuse. The links are to further resources and information on topics around domestic abuse. Download - Bright Sky App

iii. The Children's Act

The Children's Act 1989 provides a comprehensive framework for the care and protection of children. It centres on the welfare of children up to their 18th birthday. It defines parental responsibility and encourages partnership working with parents.

iii.1. Section 8 Orders

iii.1.1. Child Arrangements Orders

Section 8 of the Children's Act 1989 are orders made by the Family Court judge **to decide who the child is to live with or spend time with**, and can be granted to more than one person whether they live together or not.

iii.1.2. Residence Order

A Residence Order is an Order settling the arrangements to be made as to the person with whom the child is to live. Following a Divorce, parents will share Parental Responsibility and therefore the making of a Residence Order will only decide where a child will live. If the parties are in agreement about where a child should live, then there is no need for either party to make an application to the Court for a Residence Order.

iii.1.3. Contact Order

A Contact Order is an Order requiring the person with whom the child lives, or is to live (regardless of whether there is a Residence Order in force or not) to allow the child to visit or stay with the person named in the Order, or for that person and the child otherwise to have contact with each other. A Contact Order can authorise physical contact, but can also cover contact by letter, e-mail or by telephone. The amount of contact can either be specified in the Order or the Order could be for "reasonable contact" in which case the arrangements can be made by the parents.

iii.1.4. Prohibited Steps Order

A Prohibited Steps Order is an Order that no step that could be taken by a parent in meeting his or her Parental Responsibility for a child, shall be taken by any person without the consent of the Court. This Order deals with specific problems which have arisen. An important restriction on a Prohibited Steps Order is that it can relate only to matters which are included within Parental Responsibility.

iii.1.5. Specific Issue Order

A Specific Issue Order is an Order giving directions for the purpose of determining a specific question which has arisen or which may arise in connection with any aspect of Parental Responsibility for a child. It does not give a parent a general power, it just makes a decision on one issue over which there is a disagreement which cannot be resolved (for example sterilisation or circumcision, a course of treatment for immunisation, the religion the child should adopt and do forth).

iii.1.6. Section 8 Children Act 1989

The party wishing to apply for any of the above Orders will do so under Section 8 of the Children Act 1989. Section 1, of the above Act, states that the child's welfare shall be the Court's paramount consideration. The Welfare Principal shall determine any contested proceedings under this Act.

In applying the Welfare Principal, the Court will carefully consider a checklist which is set out below, however this is not an exhausted list and the Court can also take any other relevant factors into account:

- The ascertainable wishes and feelings of the child concerned (considered in the light of their age and understanding).
- The child's physical, emotional and educational needs.
- The likely effect on the child of any change in circumstances.
- The child's age, sex, background and any characteristics of the child which the Court considers relevant.
- Any harm that the child has suffered or is at risk of suffering.
- How capable each of the child's parents and any other person in relation to whom the Court considers the question relevant is of meeting the child's needs.

iii.1.7. The range of powers available to the Court under this Act

Where a Court is considering whether or not to make one of the Orders listed above, the Court will not make an Order/Orders unless is considers that doing so would be better for the child than making no Order at all. This is called the "No Order Presumption". This means that there is a policy that the Court will not intervene and make an Order unless it can be shown that there is a positive need and benefit to the child in doing so.

iii.1.8. Costs

Depending on your financial circumstances, you will either need to fund the application on a private basis, or you may be eligible for Public Funding (Legal Aid). Your Solicitor will advise you of this.

iii.1.9. Where the Proceedings are Issued

A Section 8 Application can either be made at a Family Proceedings Court (County Court) or at a Magistrates Court. If there are Divorce Proceedings and/or Ancillary Relief Proceedings, it is usual for a Section 8 Application to be made at a County Court.

iii.1.10. Court Procedure

The party wishing to apply for one of the above Orders, will file the necessary form at either the Family Proceedings Court or the County Court. The Court will then list the matter for what is known as a First Directions Appointment.

The task of the Court at the first appointment is to investigate the issues, enquire into the possibility of settlement and give directions in any case that has to proceed. If the matter can be settled by agreement, the terms of the agreement will be recorded in a Court document and approved by the Court. If no such agreement can be reached, the Court will make the necessary directions to progress the matter.

Sometimes these directions include both parties filing a witness statement, a CAFCASS Officer being appointed and preparing a report, the listing of the matter for a next appointment (Final Directions Appointment). If, after the CAFCASS report has been filed, the parties are still unable to agree, then at the Final Directions Appointment, the Court will set a date for the Final Hearing. The Judge will make an Order at the Final Hearing.

iii.2. Section 7 Orders

A Section 7 report **is a report written by a CAFCASS worker or a social worker** from the Local Authority in cases where an application has been made to the Family Court under Section 8 of The Children Act 1989. A Section 7 report may be required in private proceedings where an application has been made to the Court for an Order under Section 8 of The Children Act 1989, which may be:

- Child Arrangements Order - specifies whom the child is to live with and/or with whom the child is to have contact;
- Prohibited Steps Order - prevents either parent from doing certain things or making specific trips with their children without the express permission of the other parent;
- Specific Issue Order - an order to determine a specific question which has or may arise in connection with any aspect in relation to a child;
- Family Assistance Order - a short-term order requiring a CAFCASS officer or a social worker to advise, assist, and befriend any person in the named order.

A Section 7 report is ordered by the Court when they want information about a child's welfare, what is best for the child and sometimes where there are certain risk factors or concerns raised in relation to a child, parent or other relative. A CAFCASS worker or social worker will provide an independent assessment of a situation and will report these findings to the Court. The Court usually stipulates what they want the worker to focus on in their report.

iii.2.1. What will a Section 7 Report contain?

A Section 7 report needs to contain all background information, key facts and evidence that the needs of the child have been considered in accordance with the Welfare Checklist. The report will set out the child's wishes and feelings and what the CAFCASS officer Social Worker considers to be in the best interest of the child.

The person who prepares the report may speak to the child (depending on their age and understanding) about their wishes and feelings and what they would like to happen. They will also spend time with both parties and listen to any concerns they may have. They may also speak to other people such as family members, teachers and health workers. They will not ask the child to make a decision or to choose between either parent as to who they will live with and any contact they will have with the non-resident parent.

iii.2.2. If you are not happy with the Section 7 report, what can you do?

If you do not agree with the report it is important that you let the Court know your concerns. The judge will consider your concerns when making a decision.

iii.2.3. Who makes the final decision?

After reading the report and listening to what you and other people in the case have said the Court will make the final decision about what should happen to your children. The Court will make the decision based on what is best for the child. It will take into account their wishes and feelings but the order may not be in accordance with the child's wishes and feelings if this is not considered to be in their best interests. The decision will be set out in a Court Order which you must comply with.

iii.3. Section 11 Orders

Section 11 of the Children Act 2004 **places duties on a range of organisations and individuals to ensure their functions, and**

any services that they contract out to others, are discharged having regard to the need to safeguard and promote the welfare of children.

iii.3.1. Which Organisations Does this Affect?

Section 11 places a duty on:
- Local authorities and district councils that provide children's and other types of services, including children's and adult social care services, public health, housing, sport, culture and leisure services, licensing authorities and youth services;
- NHS organisations, including the NHS Commissioning Board and clinical commissioning groups, NHS Trusts and NHS Foundation Trusts;
- The police, including police and crime commissioners and the chief officer of each police force in England and the Mayor's Office for Policing and Crime in London;
- The British Transport Police;
- The Probation Service;
- Governors/Directors of Prisons and Young Offender Institutions;
- Voluntary and private sector organisations;
- Early years and child care;
- Faith organisations;
- Directors of Secure Training Centres; and
- Youth Offending Teams/Services

iii.3.2. What Should These Organisations Have in Place?

These organisations should have in place arrangements that reflect the importance of safeguarding and promoting the welfare of children, including:

- A clear line of accountability for the commissioning and/or provision of services designed to safeguard and promote the welfare of children;
- A culture of listening to children and taking account of their wishes and feelings, both in individual decisions and the development of services;
- Arrangements which set out clearly the processes for sharing information, with other professionals and with the Local Safeguarding Children Board (LSCP);
- A designated professional lead (or, for health provider organisations, named professionals) for safeguarding. Their role is to support other professionals in their agencies to recognise the needs of children, including responding to possible abuse or neglect. Designated professional roles should always be explicitly defined in job descriptions. Professionals should be given sufficient time, funding, supervision and support to fulfil their child welfare and safeguarding responsibilities effectively;
- Clear policies in line with those from the LSCP for dealing with allegations against people who work with children. An allegation may relate to a person who works with children who has:

  o Behaved in a way that has harmed a child, or may have harmed a child;
  o Possibly committed a criminal offence against or related to a child; or
  o Behaved towards a child or children in a way that indicates they may pose a risk of harm to children.

- In addition:

  o County level and unitary local authorities should have
  a Local Authority Designated Officer (LADO) to be
  involved in the management and oversight of
  individual cases. The LADO should provide advice and
  guidance to employers and voluntary organisations,
  liaising with the police and other agencies and
  monitoring the progress of cases to ensure that they
  are dealt with as quickly as possible, consistent with a
  thorough and fair process;

iii.4. Section 17 Orders (Children's Act 1989/2004)

Section 17 of the Children Act 1989 **imposes a general duty on
local authorities to safeguard and promote the welfare of
'children in need'** in their area. .The power under section 17 can be
used to support the family as a whole and to promote the
upbringing of the child within the family unit.

The Act defines a child in need as follows as:
- a child who is unlikely to achieve or maintain, or to have
  the opportunity of achieving or maintaining, a reasonable
  standard of health or development without the provision
  of services by a Local Authority; or
- a child whose health or development is likely to be
  significantly impaired; or further impaired, without the
  provision for him of such services; or
- a child is disabled

In 2004, Section 17, also stated- Children's services authorities
must produce a plan setting out the authority's strategy for

discharging their functions in relation to children and those young people for whom they will be responsible under the general duty to co-operate

iii.4.1.   Which type of support can be provided to a child in need?

The Local Authority can provide a range of services for a child in need. These can include:
- day care facilities for children under 5;
- advice, guidance and counselling;
- occupational, social, cultural and recreational activities;
- assistance for the child and family to have a holiday;
- family centres, where parents can receive family support and practical parenting advice, while children have a safe space to play;
- financial assistance, which may be in the form of a loan, a cash payment, or payment in kind, for example, vouchers for a particular shop, or an item of food, clothing or furniture;
- respite care (temporary relief care for the family, where the children are placed with a carer on a regular or one-off basis); and
- accommodation.

iii.5.   Section 37 Orders (Children's Act 1989)

By ordering a Section 37 investigation, **the Family Court is concerned about the welfare of the children.** The local authority (children services) is asked to find out whether they should apply for a **care order** (which places a child under the care of the Local Authority, otherwise known as a child "being in care") or a **supervision order** (placing a child or young person under the supervision of a local authority) or provide any other services or assistance in respect of your children.

The social worker will speak to you and will in most cases speak to the child/ren, but what they say and how they talk to the children will depend on the age of the children. A report will then be prepared by them and submitted to the court.

The social worker responsible for preparing the report will generally need to be present at Court when the application is heard - and should be prepared to give evidence in support of the information contained in the report.

iii.6.   Section 47 Orders (Children's Act 1989/2004) - Child Protection Enquiries

Section 47 of the Children Act 1989 **is very serious** and advises the local authority where a child is: Subject of an **Emergency Protection Order / Police Protection**; or they have reasonable cause to **suspect a child is suffering or is likely to suffer Significant Harm**.

The authority shall make necessary enquiries to decide whether they should take any action to safeguard or promote the child's welfare by obtaining access to the child/ren or ensure access is obtained by an authorised person.

Section 53 of the Children Act 2004 amends section 47 so that for the purposes of making a determination as to what action to take the authority shall:

- Ascertain the child's wishes and feelings about such action; and
- Give due consideration to the child's wishes and feelings.

The relevant Team Manager/Consultant Social Worker in Children's Social Care must ensure that Section 47 Enquiries are initiated when:

- A referral has been received that meets the criteria for immediate enquiries under Section 47 i.e. that a child is suffering or likely to suffer Significant Harm;
- Another child in the family has died or has been seriously injured and abuse is suspected;
- A Single Assessment of a child in need identifies that the child is suffering or is likely to suffer Significant Harm.

Once it has been decided that Section 47 enquiries are required, the Team Manager/Consultant Social Worker should ensure that:

- Checks are carried out with all relevant local agencies in order to ascertain who might have relevant information to contribute to a Strategy Discussion;
- The first Strategy Discussion takes place within 24 hours.

Strategy Discussions by telephone may occur:

- In less complex cases;
- At the initial stages of the enquiry in complex cases where time is needed in order to clarify who should attend a Strategy Meeting. In this situation the meeting should take place within a maximum of 5 working days.

Outcomes may be:

- No Further Action - Enquiries have revealed that there are no causes for concern. The child may be a Child in Need but the family do not wish for services to be provided, in which case the case will be closed;
- Family Support to be provided - Enquiries have revealed that there is no evidence that the child is suffering, or is likely to suffer, significant harm but there are needs that could be met by the provision of services either under section 17 of the Children Act 1989 or by signposting the family to another agency. The family are willing for a

package of support to be provided or continue to be provided.

iii.7. Section 91(14) Order (Children Act 1989)

Section 91(14) empowers the court to make **an order that prevents further future applications** for an order under Children's Act 1989 of any specified kind being made by the parties named in the order **without leave (permission) of the court**.

Basically this means, that if your abusive partner is continuing their harassment of you by instigating   unnecessary court proceedings (as my husband did), the judge can ban them until a date in the future. This is put in law, by the order, and should bring your stress levels down a bit!

iii.7.1. Re:L - A Law Case Study in Contact and Residence Cases

In a nutshell -'Re:L' states if a child witnesses abuse done to another, it is still classed as harm to them and the perpetrator can be prosecuted for it.
The longer version - The Court Report about a family referred to as 'Re: L' strongly influenced its thinking about the need for a greater awareness of the effects of domestic violence on children, whether as witnesses to it or as victims of it, and also of the impact of violence on resident parents.

Proper arrangements, the Report said, must be put in place to protect the child and the resident parent from physical and emotional harm. In addition, the court was profoundly influenced by a psychiatric report for the family's case by two child psychiatrists - Drs Sturge and Glaser. That Report persuaded the judges of some of the risks posed by allowing contact.

Referring to both the Sturge/Glaser Report and the Report to the Lord Chancellors' Department, Butler-Sloss (the highest-ranking female judge in the UK)observed that judges and magistrates, dealing with family cases, should be more aware of the existence and consequences of domestic violence. She noted the tendency of the courts in the past not to address allegations of violence in contact disputes because they assumed these were not relevant to deciding issues concerning the children.

She also suggested that the general principle applied by the courts that contact is in the child's best interests may have discouraged them from paying sufficient attention to the adverse effects on children of domestic violence. Citing the Sturge/Glaser Report, she asserted that violence to a partner involves a significant failure in parenting; it constitutes a failure to protect the child's carer and a failure to protect the child emotionally.

I hope you found these helpful.

Remember to seek help, it's there waiting for you.

You are not alone!

The Children's Act

"It's all been a misunderstanding"